A DIARY KEPT BY MRS. R. C. GERMON, AT LUCKNOW

First published 1870
This edition published by Lector House in 2023

ISBN: 978-93-5800-781-7

Lector House LLP
Registered Office: H. No. 96, Block C, Tomar Colony,
Burari, Delhi – 110084, India
info@lectorhouse.com
www.lectorhouse.com

A DIARY KEPT BY MRS. R. C. GERMON, AT LUCKNOW

MARIA GERMON

2023

LECTOR HOUSE LLP

A DIARY KEPT BY MRS. R. C. GERMON, AT LUCKNOW

Given to Herbert Litchfield
by Miss M A Garratt
sister of Mrs Germon
the Authoress

See note about 4 "Diary of Lucknow"

My sister never intended publishing them — but she was so continually pressed to do so by a few friends who thought it such a pity the manuscript should get lost or injured — two in particular, Mr Burham a friend here, the one who wrote his Father's Biography which I gave you — & an old Admiral an old friend here (since dead) that at last she had it done, but only for private circulation — & only she & I had the copies — I shall send one to you some day by Post & hope it will reach you all right — she wrote it entirely for my dear Mother & myself

& the report of each day is perfectly
correct – I suppose if nothing unforeseen
occurs we shall be going to London
as usual the end of May – but it
depends upon the time of the "Lucknow
Reunion" – so as to bring that within
my sisters & Colonel Germon's stay in
London – it is the old Garrison – the
officers who were shut in all the
time – & year by year the party becomes
smaller partly from some being
removed by death & others not able
perhaps to be in London at the time
when in London I shall hope to see
something of you – & with kind love
believe me your affec: Cousin
my sister & the Col. send M. A. Garrett
kind remembrances

You ask about the "Diary of Lucknow"

My sister never intended publishing them—but she was so continually pressed to do so by a few friends who thought it such a pity the manuscript should get lost or injured—two in particular, M[r] Burham a friend here, the one who wrote his Father's Biography which I gave you—& an old Admiral an old friend here (since dead) that at last she had it done, but only for private circulation—& only she and I had the copies—I shall send one to you [to]day by Post & hope it will reach you all right—she wrote it entirely for my dear mother & myself & the report of each day is perfectly correct—I suppose if nothing unforeseen occurs we shall be going to London as usual the end of May—but it depends upon the time of the "Lucknow dinner"—so as to bring that in during my sister's & Colonel Germon's stay in London—it is the old Garrison—the Officers who were shut in all the time—& year by year the party becomes smaller, partly from some being removed by death & others not able perhaps to be in London at the time. When in London I shall hope to see something of you—& with kind love believe me your affec[te] Cousin M A Garratt my sister & the Col. send kind remembrances.

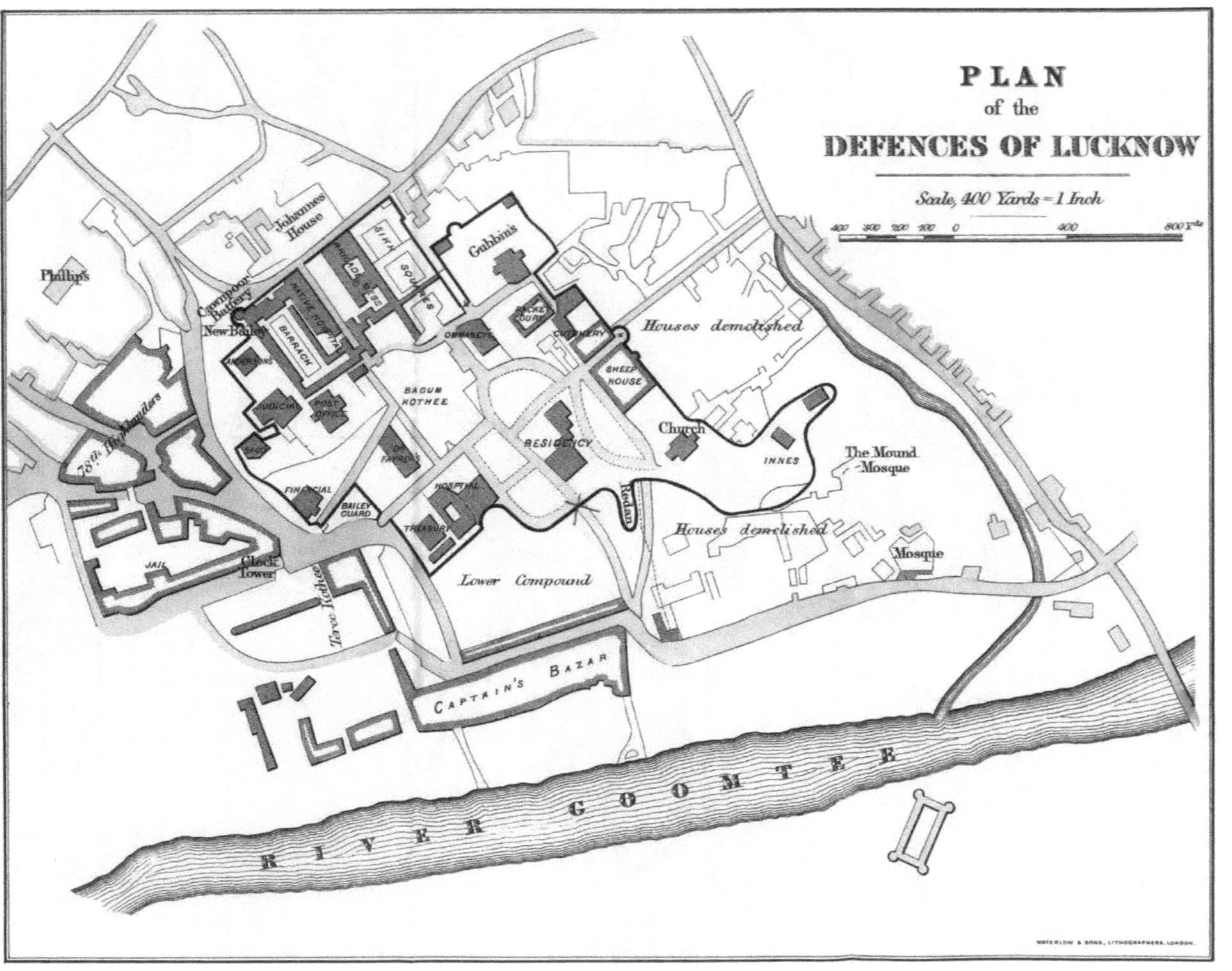

Plan of the Defences of Lucknow

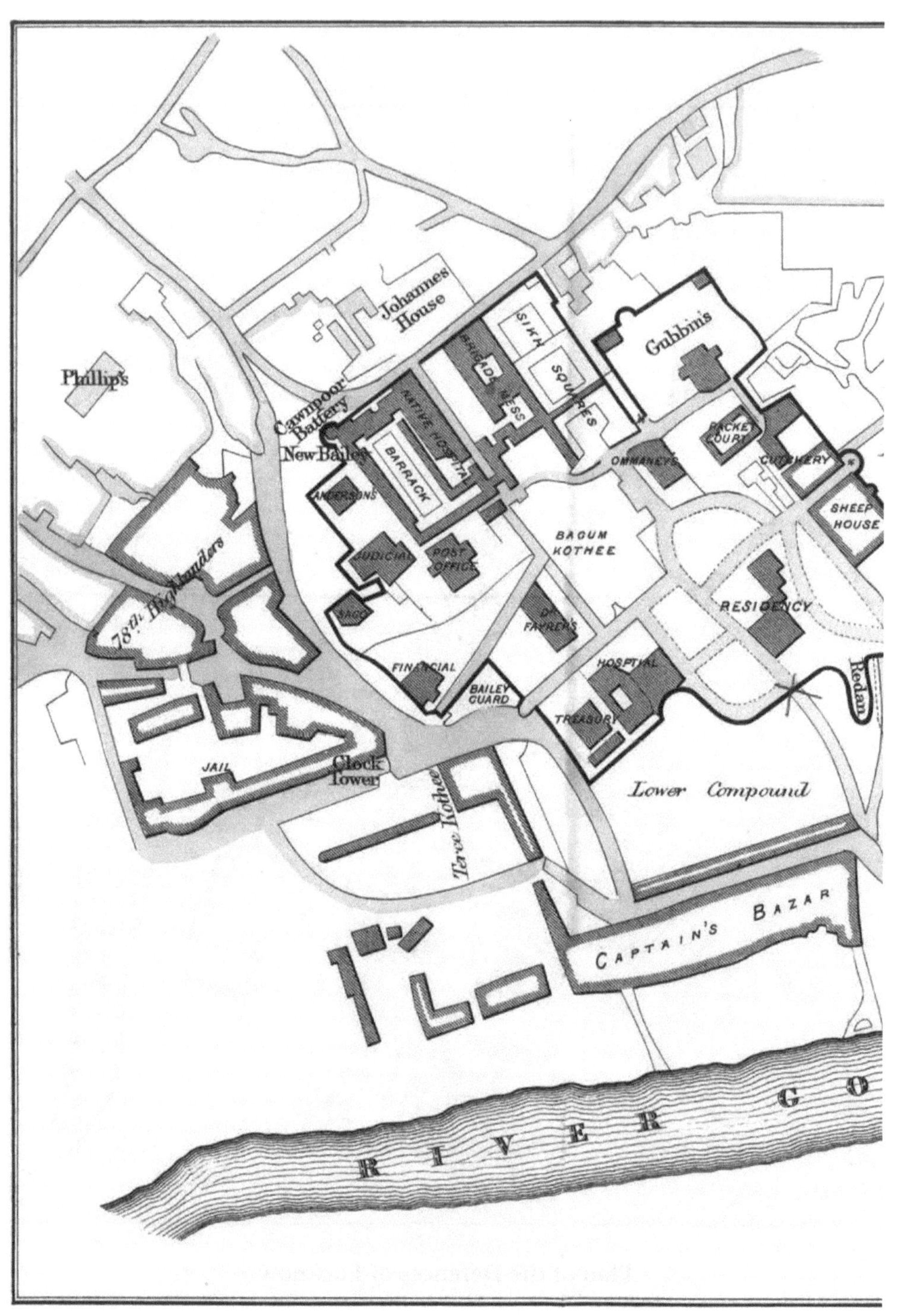

Plan of the Defences of Lucknow (*Enlarged - Left*)

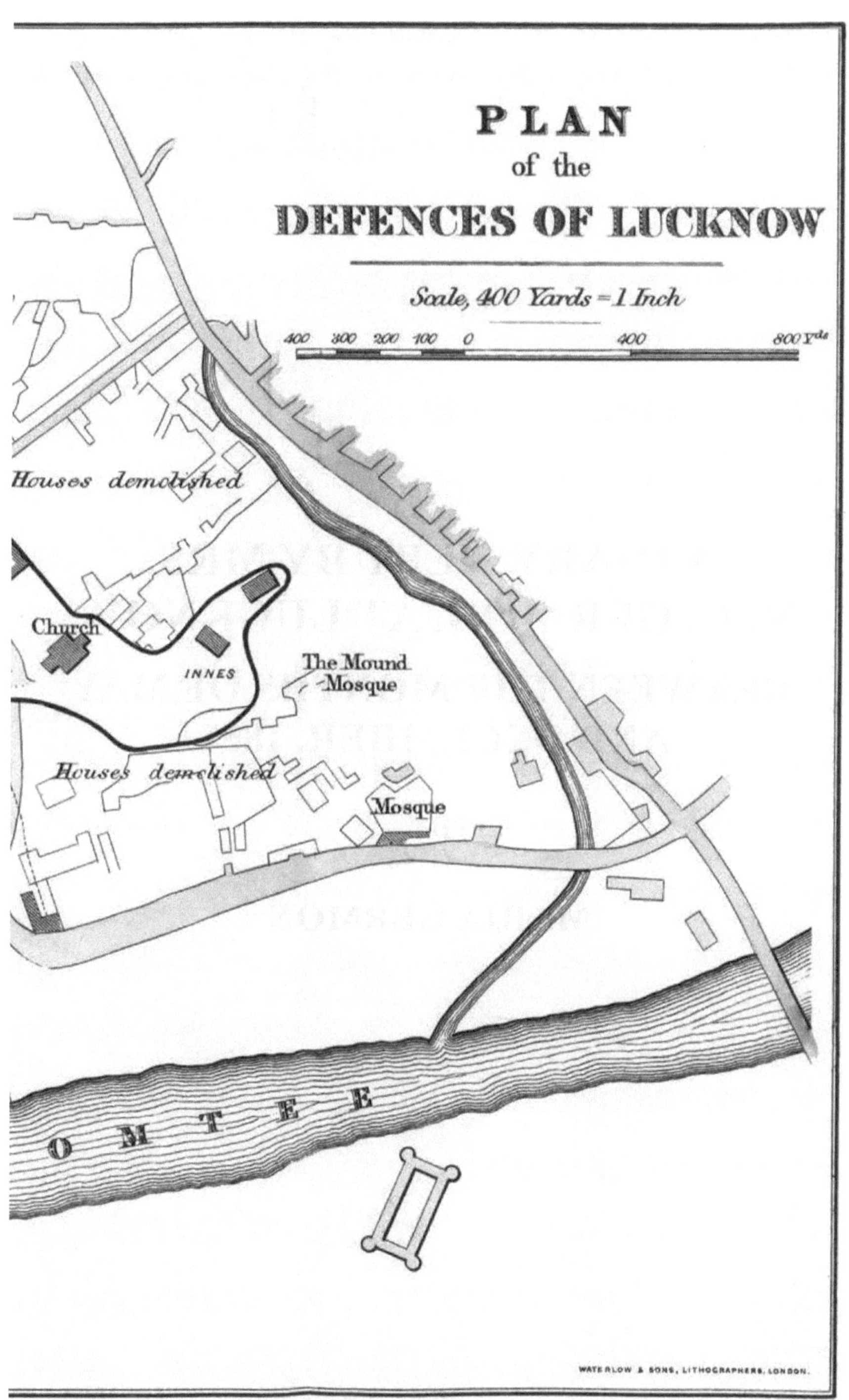

Plan of the Defences of Lucknow (*Enlarged - Right*)

A DIARY KEPT BY MRS. R. C. GERMON, AT LUCKNOW,

BETWEEN THE MONTHS OF MAY AND DECEMBER, 1857.

BY

MARIA GERMON

PREFACE.

The Writer of the following Diary has frequently been requested to have a few copies printed for circulation amongst her friends; she has now acceded to their request, but wishes it to be understood that the Diary is in its original wording, as it was written by her day by day at Lucknow, with no attempts at embellishment. The names of those who were actors in the fearful scenes have been omitted, from a feeling of delicacy towards some who are still alive.

The writer is also indebted to her husband, who commanded one of the outposts throughout the siege, for the accuracy of the statements of some of the events that did not come immediately under her own observation.

CONTENTS

Page

THE SIEGE OF LUCKNOW.

1857. May 15th, Friday. I spent the day with the B——'s of the 71st N.I., he acting Brigade-Major of Lucknow: while sitting at dinner he told us of the horrible news from Meerut and Delhi; it was rather alarming for one living alone as I was, my husband being on city duty. Mr. B—— walked home with me about half-past 8, at 9 I went to bed, taking good care to have a shawl and dressing-gown close to the bed. Charlie's orderly slept in the verandah with the servants, as he had done all the week; the B——'s had kindly offered me a bed, but I had declined it. I had one door, as usual, open close to the bedroom at which the punkah-wallah pulled the punkah; the other two were sleeping by him; the watchman, bearer, orderly, and two doggies, forming quite a guard round the door: the Ayah and her child slept in a room adjoining; and, notwithstanding the alarm, I think I never slept sounder in my life.

Saturday, May 16th. I rose soon after gun-fire, and sent off Charlie's provisions for the day, bread and butter, quail, mango-fool, and a few vegetables, and then sat in the garden and had my coffee; at 7 went into the house and prepared for a visit to the city, breakfasted at 10, and started at 11. I found Charlie had been with Sir Henry Lawrence, who was making admirable preparations in case of a rise here; Charlie said the old man was resting by a watercourse in the garden with quite a little party around him, he telling them all he knew, but advising them to spread the bad news as little as possible; and then consulting with them about precautionary measures, not objecting to a suggestion from even a captain, but catching at anything he thought good. I could see that Charlie felt perfect confidence in him; but I also saw that he thought very seriously of the state the country was in, for his remark was that we were in the position of a man sitting on a barrel of gunpowder. I sat talking with him till 1 o'clock, and then went over to the G——'s, as I had promised to spend the day with them. I found them in an awful state of alarm—talking of these murders at Delhi, and wondering if So-and-So had escaped. Miss N—— had a violent sick headache from the fright. At 2 Charlie came, and at 3 we tiffed; but Mr. G—— was so busy he could scarcely stay two minutes, and all the time was talking of the preparations. The Residency was being turned out to form a place of safety for the ladies and the sick. Charlie had to leave early to superintend arrangements also. About half-past 5 I returned to his quarters, for I longed for a little talk with him before I went home. The heat had been intense all day, and the constant talking about these murders had made me feel quite uncomfortable. Charlie was still with his guards and did not return home for some time, so I lay down quietly on his bed. I felt so nervous that, when he did return, I begged him to let me stay in a chair by him all night. However, he talked and reasoned with me and I got better. He told me two companies of the 32nd Queen's were just coming into the banquetting house, and the sick from the hospital; also a lot of women and children into some rooms under his quarters. He made me a cup of tea and then would not let me stay any longer, as it was getting dusk, and Sir Henry just driving up at the moment, I started, as Charlie had to superintend the arrival of the troops. Just outside the city my carriage had to wait to let a regiment of Irregular Cavalry pass—Captain Gr——'s. They were to be stationed at the Dawk Bungalow between the city and Cantonments, to keep up communication between the two. Instead of going home I drove to the B——'s, for I was afraid of getting nervous again, sitting by myself. They were very glad to see me and again offered me a bed, but after taking ices with them I returned, telling them in case of alarm I should rush over to them, as our bungalows adjoined each other. At home I had another cup of tea, for the heat and excitement gave one intense thirst. About 9 I went to bed, taking care to have an Affghan knife (a kind of dagger) close to me. I started at a few noises, but soon slept soundly, and fortunately heard nothing of an alarm that was given by an artilleryman of Captain Simons'—a Native—that the 13th were up in arms and were going to murder their officers. The Brigadier rode off to the lines and sent for the Adjutant and Captain Wilson, when it was discovered that the report had been caused by the preparations making for a company going off with Captain Francis to the Muchee Bawun. They walked through the lines and saw that all was right, and the Brigadier returned home; but it caused such a panic amongst some of the ladies that several rushed off to the Cantonments Residency and slept there.

Sunday, May 17th. I rose at gun-fire, and after sending off provisions to Charlie, went to church at 6, and while there seven companies of the 32nd Queen's entered Cantonments. I breakfasted at 10, and then finished my overland letters. While writing them there came a note from Mrs. A——, asking me to spend the day and night with them if I felt nervous; but I declined. Sir Henry had forty of our men (the 13th) up as a guard at the Residency, after the false report of them during the night, and told them he was perfectly satisfied with them; that he had been so much pleased with them since he had been at Lucknow that he intended writing to Calcutta and stopping all the Raviel Pindee affair. At 3 I dined, and then lay down intending to go to church, but just before the time there was an immense deal of riding and driving about, and I saw a horse battery gallop off, which I took for the European battery, that I expected something must be up in the city. I wrote off to the B——'s for news, and also sent a note off to Charlie, but I got such a headache with the start that I did not feel fit for church. It proved to be an Oude Irregular battery going off to be stationed at the Dawk Bungalow. The B——'s again pressed me to sleep at their house, although the Padre and his wife (Mr. and Mrs. Harris) were already there. While taking tea about 8, the bearer came in to tell me the subadar of Charlie's company had sent his salaam, and would send up two Sepoys to guard my house at night. I hesitated a little, but agreed at last to have them, thinking I had better not show any want of confidence in the men, although it might be a great risk in these treacherous times. However, I wrote off to Captain W——, asking if he thought they might be trusted? Captain W—— was from home, but the Adjutant wrote and said I need not hesitate—he felt perfect confidence in the men; so they came and I retired to rest, making my usual defensive preparations, and slept soundly.

Monday, May 18th. Rose at gun-fire, and while I was arranging my flowers and taking coffee in the garden, the Adjutant called to see if I were all safe—and then came a note from Mrs. P— —, saying she had heard we were to be turned out of our house to make room for the troops—and offering us two rooms. I declined, having received no orders to turn out. The Adjutant had told me the 13th mess-house had been given up to the European soldiers, and that several of the bachelors had offered their houses. About half-past 7 Charlie came home, to my great delight; the Europeans took possession of the mess-house and houses all round us, and we were well guarded: the day passed off without alarm.

Tuesday, May 19th. Charlie rose early, and went off to the lines to see after the Sepoys; on his return we went and took chota hazree (early breakfast) with the A— —'s, and heard there that Mrs. Chambers, wife of the Adjutant of the 11th N.I. had been murdered at Delhi by a butcher out of the bazaar; but that the wretch had afterwards been caught by a sweeper, and roasted alive. We are beginning to receive a few reports of the sad massacre, but at present it is not known who have perished or who have escaped; it is true that Mr. Willoughby blew up the magazine at Delhi himself. This morning a bill was found stuck on some posts in the cavalry lines, calling on all good Mussulmen to join in this rise; the cavalry brought it to their officers.[1] After breakfast came a Sepoy to Charlie to tell him that there was a panic in one of the bazaars, and that the people were all shutting up their shops and running away. Charlie went to the Brigade-Major, and soon after we saw Sir Henry drive by, and could see from our drawing-room window that the 32nd soldiers in the mess-house were all armed and accoutred, and a sergeant was stationed at the corner of the house to give the word; but after a time it subsided, and we heard the people were returning to their shops: the officer who had charge of the bazaars had been down with them, trying to make them comprehend that there was no cause for alarm. It originated in a Chuprasee (a Government servant) buying melons; he tried to get more than he ought for his money, which caused a little hubbub, and there being an order now-a-days to take up any one who makes a disturbance in the bazaar, two mounted Sepoys rode up to take him; he rushed off crying out "Shut your shops! shut your shops!" and the poor frightened wretches did it without question; the man was made prisoner, and so it ended. I have only named it to show the state of excitement we were in. While this was occurring, Capt. W— — came in and brought us a budget of Delhi news, written down by the Allyghur magistrate; it is said a party of officers were seen going into Kurnaul, eighty miles north of Delhi; so it is possible they may be fugitives from Delhi—I trust so. Captain W— — also told us that Brigadier H— — was under arrest at Meerut. There must have been great delay and mismanagement there, for the insurgents were in Meerut all Sunday night, burning and murdering, and did not reach Delhi till 4 o'clock the Monday morning. Captain W— — complimented me on my remaining alone in the house during the panic; Charlie also seems well pleased that I have done so. In the evening we took our usual drive; our

[1] This regiment afterwards mutinied to a man.

band was playing at the band-stand, but very few were driving about. We went to bed in peace—Charlie having his double-barrelled gun, loaded with a charge of shot, by the bedside; he says it is more useful than a bullet, for it would disable several, whereas a bullet might miss altogether: my weapon is the Affghan dagger, just suited to me, being neither too large nor heavy. I only trust we may have no occasion to use them, but one cannot be too guarded in these treacherous times.

Wednesday, May 20th. Charlie went off before gun-fire with Captain W— — to the city to see the Muchee Bawun, where Captain F— — is stationed. He is there with two companies of Natives, and there are also two Queen's officers and seventy men, also two guns in position besides field pieces, one to sweep the whole entrance street of Lucknow, the other the iron bridge; and then there are some Oude Irregular troops: an Engineer officer was making the place habitable for them. While there, Sir Henry drove up, and scolded first this one, and then that, and then away again to superintend some other arrangements. The day passed off without alarm. At the band in the evening Charlie went over to the G— —'s carriage, and heard that the Sappers (Natives) sent from Koorkee to Meerut, had proved treacherous, but that they had suffered severely for it, for in the same regiment was also a great number of Europeans, who had killed and wounded great numbers of them. He also heard that the Commander-in-Chief was marching down to Delhi, that he was at Kurnaal on the 18th; that he would have eight European regiments, and that he was bringing with him all the officers who had gone on leave to Simlah. Delhi is on the Grand Trunk road from Simlah.

Thursday, May 21st. While Charlie was dressing, just after gun-fire, to go and inspect his company, there came a notice round that all officers were to assemble at Sir Henry's at half-past 6. It was to inform them that he (Sir Henry) had been made Brigadier-General in Oude; that he had all power entirely in his own hands to reward or punish as he should think fit, without appealing to any higher power whatever—the finest thing that could have been done, and we cannot be too thankful for having such a man over us. Last night a light was put into one of our Native officer's huts, but fortunately, it was put to leeward. No doubt the intention was for the fire to be carried to some bungalow; but one of our Sepoys saw it, and ran and pulled it off and smothered it, burning his hands in doing so—but it looked well of the man. The day passed without alarm, but at the band, our Doctor came up to the buggy, requesting us to take his wife and child in for the night, as he said there was going to be a rise. We went home and turned out Charlie's room for her, and placed a bed in it. Just as we were sitting at tea, the servants came running in giving an alarm of fire, and when we went out we saw the flames rising up from, apparently, the next bungalow to ours but one. The wind was high, and lay in the quarter to blow the sparks to us; Charlie sent several of the servants up on our thatched roof, each with a gurra of water. We quite looked for a disturbance now. Charlie took his double-barrelled gun, and told me, if there were any, to take my Affghan knife and escape at the back of the house over the garden wall to the Residency—it is only about four feet. There is only the road between us and the Residency, the garden wall of which is about five feet, but I could manage both with a chain. However, all seemed quiet, and, fortunately, it was the stables of a house which, being tiled, the sparks were not thrown up so high as they would have been from thatch, and in about an hour and a half we saw it subside. Then came the Doctor and his family, in a fearful state of mind. We tried to quiet them, for really we did not fear much now, the fire having passed off without any rising; it was a good sign, and several of our Sepoys had come to see if our house was all right. After arranging Mrs. P— —'s room, Charlie and I went to bed; it was past 10, and he was asleep in a few minutes. I listened for a time thinking I heard noises in the Bazaar, but soon fell asleep, and the night passed without further alarm.

Friday, May 22nd. Charlie went into the garden early, just as Sir Henry was passing. Sir Henry called to him, and told him to go and learn all he could about the fire, and whether the Sepoys worked to put it out, and to come over to him at 7, when he would be back from the city. I found my visitors had had a good night, so they dressed and went home, and are to come again to-night. There are fourteen ladies sleeping at the Residency here in Cantonments every night.

Saturday, May 23rd. The day passed without alarm, excepting that in the afternoon I was by myself and heard such a tremendous noise that I was quite frightened. It turned out to be at our mess-house. The Colonel of the 32nd would have the thatched roof well saturated with water in case of fire, and in the midst of it all a fire-engine rattled up from the city (the first I ever saw in India), and in my alarm I took it for a gun.

Sunday, May 24th. We went to church early, and the day passed off quietly.

Monday, May 25th. We were aroused at 3 A.M. by a message coming for Charlie to go over to Sir Henry. He dressed and went over immediately. I waited till gun-fire, and then went into the garden to arrange my flowers, little thinking what was coming. Charlie came back about half-past 5, when, to my astonishment, he told me it was Sir Henry's express orders that all ladies should leave Cantonments and go down to the Residency in the city; so I suspected he had heard bad news.[2] I commenced immediately collecting what I thought I should require, and what I considered valuable, not knowing how long I should be from home. The heat was intense, and I had to hurry my packing, for Charlie had had an offer of a seat in the H— —'s carriage for me, as he could not take me down himself, being Captain of the week; and they were to call for me at half-past 7. He made me take some coffee, and packed up what he could of eatables and drinkables, not knowing how we should fare at the Residency. At the appointed time the H— —'s and Mrs. B— — called for me, and we drove to the city, passing innumerable coolies with beds and baggage of all descriptions, carriages and buggies filled with ladies and children, all off to the city—such a scene—and when we drove up to the Residency everything was looking so warlike, guns pointed in all directions, and barricades and European troops; everywhere nothing but bustle and confusion. We then heard there was hardly a room to be had—ladies had been arriving ever since gun-fire—so Mr. H— — went over to see if Dr. F— — could take us in. He came back saying he could, and away we went, thankful to get into such good quarters. Two ladies were there already, and five came after, with three children, so that every room

[2] The Cawnpore troops were expected to rise, and then we had but little chance of remaining quiet ourselves.

was full. This house, as well as Mr. G——'s and Mr. O——'s (both also full) are within the Residency grounds, and are barricaded all round; still, in case of disturbance, we have orders to assemble at the Residency. Of course, there are all kinds of reports and alarms going about consequent on our flight. The heat was intense; I never experienced anything like it: at night it is fearful, I cannot sleep for it. Our beds are three under one punkah. I and Mrs. A—— are with Mrs. F—— in her room. In the other rooms they are as crowded, but it is nothing to the Residency. Our party here is a very agreeable one. We meet at chota hazree, and, after dressing, breakfast at 10. We then have working, reading and music—there are some very good performers amongst our party—lunch at 2, dine at half-past 7, and then the Padre reads a chapter and prayers, and we retire.

Tuesday, May 26th. The day passed quietly. Several husbands and fathers visited their beloveds, but mine could not leave his station duty. In the evening I went to the Residency to see Mrs. B——, whose baby was dying. I never witnessed such a scene—a perfect barrack—every room was filled with six or eight ladies; beds all round, and perhaps a dining-table laid for dinner in the centre—servants thick in all the verandahs—numbers of the 32nd soldiers and their officers; and underneath all, the women and children of the 32nd barracks—such a hubbub and commotion! It is an upper storeyed house, but the upper storey is not nearly so large as the under one, and yet in that, including servants and children, there are ninety-six people living! Poor Mrs. B—— was in great distress; she and another lady had a small room to themselves, with her five children. I was quite thankful I was not there: it was a complete rabbit warren. On my return I found Dr. F—— and Mr. H—— had been to Cantonments, and heard that the 13th Sepoys had taken up four city men, one of whom attempted to stab Mr. C——, the Adjutant.

Wednesday, May 27th. The day passed quietly. I went over to the Residency to see Mrs. P—— and Mrs. A—— in the evening, and found them in a small room with another lady. Mrs. P——'s child had bad fever—it was such a scene—they were having a punkah put up, and their beds were so thick you could hardly move, and scarcely a breath of air to be had. Such a hubbub all round—some parties were grouped in a circle in the verandah, some in the compound—but it is impossible to describe the scene; I can compare it to nothing but a rabbit warren.

Thursday, May 28th. The day passed as usual. In the evening two of us drove with Dr. and Mrs. F—— to the Martinière College, he taking with him a very small pistol, and concealed from view, on the coach-box, a double-barrelled gun. The part of the city we drove through seemed perfectly quiet.

Friday, May 29th. About 5 A.M. I drove with Miss H—— to Cantonments, and had the inexpressible delight of seeing Charlie again, and the poor doggies I thought would have eaten me up. I had chota hazree with Charlie, and we sat chatting till 7, when the H——'s carriage came for me again. The day passed quietly. Some of the party drove out with Dr. and Mrs. F——, in the evening, but I did not. Dr. F——'s elephant is brought every evening to the verandah, where we are generally all assembled, to have his dinner. He has large cakes made of 32lbs. of ottah (coarse flour). This evening he performed various feats: taking the Mahout upon his back by his trunk, then putting out his forepaw for the Mahout to climb up that way; roaring, when he was told to speak, and then salaaming and taking his departure.

Saturday, May 30th. I went down to Cantonments again with Miss H——, and Col. H—— told us if we liked to remain till 11, he would take us back to the city himself. I was glad to accede to it, but it was against orders, for we are only allowed to go down to Cantonments morning and evening, and stay two hours. I enjoyed my time with Charlie; had a delightful bath, and appreciated the luxury of my own bathing and dressing rooms; then breakfasted with Charlie, who did not like my remaining in Cantonments so long against orders. The poor doggies were wild—"Prince," a little Scotch terrier, seemed to think himself privileged to be saucy as his mistress had come to see him, and got away under a sofa, and growled, and bid defiance to the servant who came to take him away to be washed, so that Charlie had to come to the rescue. However, the whole time Charlie was in a fidget about my remaining against orders. At 11 the carriage came. I little thought it was my last sight of the pretty garden and the home I had spent so many happy hours in, and of my poor little doggies. After taking up Col. H—— and his daughter, who should we meet but Sir H. Lawrence, returning from the city; and he stared me full in the face. I was in terror, for I feared Charlie would get a wigging for letting me remain so long in Cantonments, and he is always so particular not to disobey orders. The day passed quietly. The elephant came to the verandah to be fed, and we sat down to dinner, laughing and talking—quite a merry party—when, about 9, the servants came running in, saying there was a great deal of firing going on in the direction of Cantonments. We all started up. Dr. F—— and Mr. H—— rushed off to discover the truth of it, and sure enough there was artillery and musketry plainly to be heard, and from the top of the house tremendous fires could be seen blazing up. Dr. F—— at first ordered us to get our bonnets and go to the Residency; then he said we had better go down to the underground part of the house: and he had all the doors locked, and they armed themselves. It was an awful time for us who had our husbands in Cantonments, for there was not a doubt but that the Native troops had risen, and were burning and murdering. Dr. F—— then told us to get together a little bundle of linen, and what we might require in case we were ordered off to the Muchee Bawun—we might be kept there some time—but it must be only a small bundle, that we could carry in our hands. We did so, and then all collected in the dining-room, awaiting our orders, Mrs. F——'s baby asleep in the midst of us; the suspense was fearful. About 2, came down Mr. J——, the commissariat officer, with a message from Sir Henry, that the Native troops had risen, but that we had held our own, and the rebels had fled. Dr. F—— then said we had better all go and lie down in our clothes, with our bundles ready, and he would call us if there were any further alarm. We went; but I could only walk up and down the room, thinking of Charlie, and whether he had been wounded. Mrs. F—— gave me a cup of tea, and while I was drinking it they came running in to tell me Charlie was all right. He had ridden up with a despatch from Sir Henry for Mr. G——, escorted by twenty Irregular Cavalry men, and a few minutes after he made his appearance. I never shall forget the moment. I could only thank God he was safe. His trowsers, up to the knees, were covered with blood, but it was from his horse having been shot in the nose. He himself had had a most narrow escape; the Brigadier was shot about two yards from him. Of course all the ladies in the house crowded round him, and his first words were, "All belonging to the ladies in this house are safe." He then mentioned the Brigadier's death, and Mr. G——'s, of the 71st N.I.; also, that Mr. C—— had been wounded in the leg. They had just brought him down to the Residency, in Sir Henry's carriage. I could only shudder to think what an escape my own dear husband had had. He said they were sitting at mess when the alarm was given, and that he rushed off to the Brigadier, being his orderly officer that week. The Brigade-Major joined them, and they went into the Lines, when the Sepoy of the 13th, who had been rewarded a few days previously, and who was carrying the Brigadier's gun, called out, "Save yourself, Sahib; they are going to fire!" A volley was fired, but the Brigadier was not hit then. Charlie was on foot; he had tried to mount a horse of Capt. W——'s, but it had thrown him—most fortunately for him as it turned out afterwards—then went on again and received another volley, and then a third, and Charlie says it was most marvellous they were not hit. They had then reached the European camp, when the Brigadier would go a little further, although the soldiers warned him not to. A shot immediately struck him in the breast, and he fell from his horse like a stone—quite dead. Charlie ordered some European soldiers to carry him into camp, which they did; and he said it was only from not being mounted himself that he was not hit—they fired too high. He and Mr. B—— rushed off, and Charlie's groom met him in the bazaar with his horse. He lost Mr. B—— in the bazaar, but dared not wait; they were all in arms around him. It was the 71st N.I. that commenced the mutiny—they rushed off and got their arms, and the bad ones of the other regiments joined them. However, the great guns settled them, and they made off into the district. Sir Henry then asked who would carry down a despatch to the city, and Charlie offered, for he thought of me, so he galloped off with his twenty Sowars,[3] leaving the bungalows burning on all sides of him. He fancied not one would escape. Ours for that night did, owing to Charlie's orderly telling the party of the 48th, who had come to burn it, that there was a Havildar's party inside, who would fire instantly; so they passed on to the next. This man got 100 rupees afterwards from Sir Henry for this. Charlie did not go back to Cantonments that night, as his horse was quite done up, and he had had leave to do as he liked. He went back to Mr. G——, and we all went to bed. Never shall I forget this awful night, nor how much I have to thank God for having preserved my dear one.

Sunday, May 31st. Charlie came over to breakfast with us; we all then went into Dr. F——'s room, and Mr. H—— read prayers; Charlie then went to see if Sir Henry had arrived, and I wrote my overland letters and was just closing them, when an order came for all ladies to go over to the Residency, as they expected a rise in the city; we collected our bundles, and, under a burning sun, walked over to the Residency, where we were told not to congregate too many in one part, as the building was not safe; every room in the upper storey was crammed, we could hardly get space to put down our bundles: at last Miss N—— offered me a corner in one room, but the perfect Babel there was with the number of children and the fearful heat, with no punkahs going, was enough to drive one wild. We sat down

[3] These all turned against us afterwards.

in this miserable state all day; there was luncheon going on when we arrived, and we were invited to partake, but Mrs. F— — kindly sent over for one from her own house for us. I saw my husband every now and then, but he was acting under Major A— —. In the evening the two Padres tried to have prayers, but we could scarcely hear them from the Babel of tongues all round and the screams of so many children; it was perfect misery. I was dying with thirst, and had nothing of my own to quench it; at last a lady took pity on me, and ordered her servant to make me a cup of tea—a perfect luxury. We heard firing going on all the evening; it turned out to be an attack on the Dowlut Khana, but the rebels were repulsed, several shot, and others taken prisoners, who were afterwards hanged. Martial law is proclaimed now in Oude, so they are hanging several night and morning at the Muchee Bawun. About 7, Sir Henry came down from Cantonments with a large escort, and was received with great cheering; four more guns came down with him; every preparation was made, expecting an attack that night; every man was at his gun, and the slow matches lighted in readiness. There was no chance of sleeping down in this hot Babel, so I and several other ladies took our bedding up on the roof and slept there; it was a lovely moonlight night, and never shall I forget the scene. The panorama of Lucknow, from the top of the Residency, is splendid; and down immediately below us, in the compound, we could see the great guns and all the military preparations; all, every instant, expecting an attack, and firing going on in the distance. However, I was so worn out with the previous night that I lay down and was asleep in a second; of course I did not undress, nor had I done so the night before. I started frequently, fancying I heard the tramp of the mob coming; we had the two Padres up with us and they determined to watch by turns. Mr. P— — began; he had a double-barreled gun, pistol and sword, and walked round and round for two hours, and then awoke Mr. H— —, but we could not help laughing, for Mr. H— — was so sleepy he told him he did not think there was any necessity for watching up there. I shall never forget the night; the moon and stars were so brilliant overhead, looking so peaceful in contrast to the scene below. I fixed up an umbrella over my head to keep off the ill effects of the moon; every hour the sentinels were calling to one another and answering, "All's well!" It was certainly more a scene from romance than real life. Sir Henry slept out, like the others, between two guns.

Monday, June 1st. As soon as it was light, I rolled up my bundle of bedding and went down to find Charlie; he was just going off to Cantonments with Sir Henry, being made Acting Adjutant in the room of Mr. C— —, and they have all orders to remain in camp in Cantonments; so I must not expect to see him now. The heat is fearful in tents by day—there are two or three companies of Europeans and some guns, and all the Native troops who remained staunch to us, encamped together; our treasure and regimental colours are saved; the former entirely by Mr. L— —'s bravery. One is hearing now of the wonderful escapes some of the officers had that night; the only wonder is that so many escaped; numbers have lost their all. To continue. Mrs. F— — gave me a cup of tea: one's thirst is fearful in this intense heat and excitement; I contrived to send a cup down to Charlie. Poor fellow! he has not undressed at night for more than a week; he went back in Sir Henry's carriage, for his own horse is quite done up. Just as I was wondering where I should find a corner to dress in, Dr. F—— gave us notice that we might go back to his house, for he thought it safer than the Residency, with that crowd; it was perfect paradise to get back again, and I had a lovely bath. I could not do much throughout the day, for I was overpowered with drowsiness; we had no alarms: at night we hardly liked undressing, but I thought it would rest one more, so I put on a thick dressing-gown and placed my bundle ready and fell asleep. We were aroused by a slight alarm, but it ended in nothing. I partly dressed, and lay down again. It was occasioned by a sick man, in his delirium, calling out "Murder!" However, it caused a great commotion, and every one was ordered to arm himself; it only shows what an excited state we are all in.

Tuesday, June 2nd. The day passed quietly. In the evening Mr. C—— paid me a visit, and gave many particulars of that awful night; he is come down on city duty.

Wednesday, June 3rd. The first news we heard from without was the death of the Commander-in-Chief, from cholera, at Umballah; then about 1 o'clock came Major B—— and Mr. P—— to tell the F——'s Dr. F——'s brother had been killed by the insurgents; it was a day of bad news: also poor Captain H——, who has left a widow and seven children, and Mr. B——, a newly-married man. I believe they removed poor Mrs. H—— to Mrs. G——'s before telling her the sad news. As I and Mrs. A—— occupied Mrs. F——'s room, we offered to give it up to her and her husband, but they would not hear of it; we had no further alarm in the city.

Thursday, June 4th. I rose as soon as it was light, to get a little air; the heat is so intense in this house that this is the only breath of air one gets in the day. While sitting in the garden, fifty Europeans of the 84th arrived in dawk carriages, Dr. P—— and Major G—— with them. Major G——'s regiment had mutinied, and they had with difficulty escaped with their lives. Dr. P—— said they expected an attack between this and Cawnpore, so as there were four soldiers to each carriage, two always kept watch outside with their muskets loaded, and the carriages were kept all together. Poor Mrs. F—— was looking out her mourning; it seemed so sad that neither she nor Dr. F—— had a room to themselves. After dinner news was brought that the 41st N.I. at Setapore had mutinied, and that the ladies and gentlemen were flying, so Dr. F—— and Mr. G—— sent off their carriages immediately to meet them; a party of gentlemen had ridden off already, and Dr. F—— and Dr. P—— followed them. At sunset I went over with Mr. C—— to see Mrs. A—— and Mrs. P——; the latter is in great distress for clothing, having lost everything the night of the mutiny, like many others. While I was sitting with them, the fugitives drove in, bringing in news that Colonel B——, the commandant of the 41st, had been shot by his men; his poor daughter was with the fugitives: there were many missing, and it was afterwards known that all living in or near the Civil Lines perished, excepting Sir M—— J—— and his sister, who formerly resided here with their uncle, Mr. C. C. J——, the chief commissioner.

Friday, June 5th. Rose at gun-fire, for the heat is so unbearable I am glad to get up. Several of the 32nd officers joined us while we were sitting in the garden, and the discussion was, why the hanging should be stopped? There has been none the last two days, and before that they were hanging six or eight morning and evening in front of the Muchee Bawun. The day passed without alarm. In the evening, to our surprise, we heard the remainder of the 48th N.I. were ordered to Deriowbad for treasure; of course we concluded it was a great risk for the officers, although they are the Sepoys that remained staunch at the mutiny. It is quite risk enough being with them in Cantonments with only a handful of Europeans. I went over to see Mrs. B— —, who is in great distress, having just lost her baby. She told me of her narrow escape the night of the mutiny in the Cantonments; she was down there with all her children, although Sir H. L— — had forbidden ladies to be there at night. She told me, she and the Major were in bed when a Havildar came rushing in, begging her to fly, for the Sepoys were up in the Lines, and immediately after the mutineers came to the house and asked for the Sahib and Mem-Sahib; she fled with her five children, escorted by three friendly Sepoys, first into the servants' houses, but the bullets came whistling so thick that the Sepoys cut a hole in the mud-wall for her to escape at the back. They fled to a village, but the villagers came out and threatened to take their lives if they remained, so they went and took refuge in a dry nullah (a bed of a stream); it was about fifteen or twenty feet deep, so that they had to sit and slide down the bank; the Sepoys lay down on the bank and watched; her poor baby had dysentery, and had nothing on but its night-clothes: no wonder it died a day or two after; but, then, she ought not to have been in Cantonments. She drove up to the city next day, but Sir Henry was so angry with her for having disobeyed his orders that he would not allow her an escort. Mrs. M— —, the Pension Paymaster's wife, has lost everything—she says 50,000 rupees' worth of property—for the bungalow was their own, and being stationary at Lucknow, they had everything in the greatest luxury; she had an immense amount of jewellery. Miss N— — spent the day with us.

Saturday, June 6th. Another quiet day. I had a great fright in the afternoon, for a fire was seen in Cantonments. However, I got a note from Charlie, saying all was quiet; the 71st Lines had been burnt down.

Sunday, June 7th. Rose at gun-fire, and went to church with nearly all our party, for Sir Henry said it was quite safe. The church is in the entrenchment. We stayed to the Sacrament, and it was quite comforting. The day passed quietly. Most attended service again in the evening, for there were sentries round the church; but the heat was so extreme I felt unequal to going.

Monday, June 8th. A quiet day. Firing has been heard for two days at Cawnpore. In the evening a Mrs. A— —, of the 41st, a fugitive from Setapore, called and gave a description of the mutiny there; and a Mr. V— — came in and reported he had seen the bodies of Mrs. C— — and the two Miss J— —'s lying in the road.[4]

Tuesday, June 9th. Another quiet day; no news. I went to see Mrs. A— —, who had been very ill, but was better. Mrs. F— — went to several of the ladies from Secroara, who are living in the Begum Kotee (another house in the Residency compound for the accommodation of the ladies) and told me she had seen Mrs. B— — and Mrs. K— —; they were without even a change of clothes. I think they came in from Secroara with the Setapore party; Mrs. B— — had not even a change for her baby! They are still going on making our entrenchment stronger and stronger; two

[4] Not true.

18-pounders have been put in position, for the insurgents have guns at Cawnpore from the Rajah of Bhitoor,[5] who has joined them. We dine now at 4 o'clock, and have tea and ices in the garden in the evening; and, we are in luxury, compared with most.

Wednesday, June 10th. Went into the garden early, and heard that some women and children had been brought in from Setapore in dhoolies (palanquins for the sick) led by a sergeant who had his arm in splinters. They brought a frightful account of the atrocities committed there—too barbarous and inhuman to be mentioned. I sent plates, cups and saucers, &c., &c., to the Secroara ladies, and linen to poor Mrs. B——. We were told, at breakfast, that we must not be alarmed if we heard a great explosion, for they were going to blow up a gateway near us. They are clearing as much as they can, a space around us, to give as little cover as possible for the enemy to fire from, in case it comes to a siege. In the evening, I and several others went over to the Begum's house, and saw Mrs. K—— and Mrs. B——; the place was very dirty, but the room lofty and good. Mrs. F—— brought away Mrs. B—— and four children to our house.

Thursday, June 11th. The atrocities committed at Setapore are beyond belief; a whole heap of babies was found,—the poor little creatures bayonetted and thrown on a heap. The ladies from Deriowbad came in, and Mr. B——, an artillery officer, from Secroara; his artillerymen (Natives) made him come in, and actually gave him fifty rupees for expenses on the road: so the rebels have his guns. A sergeant-major, from Setapore, brought news that the treasury there had been plundered, and that the rebels had then started for Gondah, intending to loot that also. The poor ladies from Setapore and Gondah were in a dreadful state about their husbands. I settled my Kitmagar's account, and paid a few rupees to each of the servants. Mrs. F—— was taking in stores all day, in case of a siege. The explosion was expected this day, as it was a failure yesterday. In the evening I paid another visit to the ladies in the Begum's house.

Friday, June 12th. Captain W—— came over, and said the Sepoys were to be sent to their homes and the officers from Cantonments to come down here; this was good news indeed. Mr. G—— sent over to say that a messenger was going off to Benares in disguise and would take a small letter for each of us and try and post them there, as our last overlands were still lying at the post-office, the road having been closed for some days. We all commenced writing immediately, one sheet each, and when they were sent over, Mr. G——, to our great disgust, said they were all too large, and that we could only send a piece one quarter of the size; so we commenced again, and the puzzle then was how to fold so small a piece for overland passage. Soon after, while arranging with my servants and taking my Kitmagar's account for May, I heard two muskets fired and some of the great guns gallop off. I could hardly sit still, but I did not like the men to see me frightened. I finished the Kitmagar's account and paid it, but I must own he might have cheated me. When I went back into the drawing-room I found it was the police had mutinied. Soon after, the gentlemen came home and said the police had bolted, but two guns and a company of Europeans had gone after them; also a body of

[5] The Nana.

gentlemen on horseback. In the evening I went over to see Mrs. A— —, who was up for the first time. On my return, we had tea and ices in the garden, and while sitting there the guns and infantry returned bringing news that forty of the enemy had been killed and many taken prisoners. Three of the Europeans had fallen out by the way from the intense heat, and one had died from apoplexy. Two of our Sikhs were killed; and Mr. T— —, a civilian, had been wounded by a bayonet in his shoulder; he walked in while we were there, and Dr. F— — took him into his room and dressed the wound. We all retired for the night. Mr. E— —, 32nd Queen's, came in for a moment in passing, but appeared quite done up; he threw himself into a chair, and had a glass of soda-water, and told us that they and the guns had not been able to get up with the enemy; he told us, afterwards, he had been obliged to have leeches on his temples that same night.

Saturday, June 13th. Rose early, and wrote to Charlie I expected my piano up from Cantonments, as Mrs. F— — had offered to take it in. About 7, I went in to dress and bathe, and while there Captain W— — called and sent to say he must see me—no one else could give me his message—he must see me himself. I quickly dressed and threw on a shawl and received him in Mrs. F— —'s little room; it was to tell me that Charlie would be down at half-past 4, as the regiment was coming, but I was to say nothing about it till they arrived. After that, they brought me news that my piano was not allowed to pass the gate. I wrote Captain G— —, who refused to let it pass, and then to Major A— —, who said it was a peremptory order that no furniture could be taken into the entrenchments, but he very kindly offered to take it into his own house for me in the Teree Kotie, just outside; I, however, sent it to the Martinière. The day passed quietly, and about 6 came dear Charlie; he could not stay long, for he had engaged to dine with Sir Henry: however, he first sent off the buggy and two great boxes of property, which he had had brought up from Cantonments to the Martinière.

Sunday, June 14th. I rose early to see Charlie, and then went to church at 7. The day was quiet, but word was brought that Captain B— — and Mr. F— — of the 48th N.I., and Captain S— —, and Mr. B— — of the 7th Cavalry, all out on detachment duty, had been murdered by their men. Charlie came again in the evening, and I had a nice chat with him.

Monday, June 15th. Charlie came again, and promised another visit in the evening. My Ayah also came, and seemed overjoyed to see me; it was agreed that she and her family should have a house in the bazaar: the only drawback was, that now something must be done with the poor doggies, and they were under their charge. Poor Prince had such a sore back from the heat, living in the tents with Charlie, that Charlie had bought strychnine to give them before he came away, but had not the heart to do it. At 11, in came Charlie, unexpectedly, to say he had been ordered off to the Muchee Bawun with his Sikhs. I was greatly disappointed, hoping to have had him here. It was agreed that the poor pets were to be sent to him to the Muchee Bawun to be killed. I felt so wretched all day, and the heat was intense—all was quiet.

Tuesday, June 16th. The first news we heard was, that Major G— —, who had gone off in disguise with despatches, had been betrayed by his men—ten of his own selecting—and killed at Roy Bareilly; and while we were at breakfast, Captain W— — brought news that a letter had come by a messenger from General W— — at Cawnpore, dated the 14th, 11 o'clock. They had held out till then, but had lost a great number of men—Captain W— — would not say how many—so I fear it was very bad news. The Ayah came, and the poor doggies were taken to Charlie. I had not the heart to take a last look at them. Charlie and the cook drowned them in the river. Poor Charlie! it was hard for him to have to do it. The day passed quietly, but bad news was arriving from the district constantly. Mrs. B— — and some others killed at Sultanpore. She in a Rajah's fort!—but one hears now of nothing but wholesale massacres! Charlie came in the evening, and it did my heart good to see him.

Wednesday, June 17th. We heard to-day of Mr. C— —, the civilian, being killed; he was engaged to Miss D— —; her wedding things had arrived just before these troublous times, and the marriage had been postponed. We heard that Mr. B— —, of the 48th, had been shot in the trenches at Cawnpore; his servant brought in the news. News was also brought that the Futteyghur people, 160 in number, had been murdered on the parade ground at Cawnpore, in sight of our people. They were going down the river in boats, but were stopped and taken to Cawnpore and there blown from guns. The day was quiet here. They are building a wall up against our windows to keep off musket shots; it is loop-holed, also, for our troops in case of necessity. The Fyzabad Rajah has joined the rebels, and is said to be very near us with his guns. Charlie came early in the evening.

Thursday, June 18th. I paid my bearer his account, and he went off to be with Charlie. Major B— — came in several times. All garrison officers were ordered to their posts this morning, to receive orders what they are to do when the enemy arrives. The Martinière boys were brought in. Just before breakfast, the groom brought me seven rupees, saying he had sold the poor buggy horse. I felt much inclined for a good cry; I have driven him myself so often. We were obliged to sell him. Charlie came about half-past 6; one of his Sikhs had taken an immense quantity of churrus, and become quite frenzied, and then stabbed another Sikh; they called on him to put down his arms, or he would be shot, and he threw down his musket with such force that he broke it in pieces; the other poor man died.

Friday, June 19th. A quiet day. Charlie could not come to see me, as he was on duty at one of the gates of the Muchee Bawun; there are five gates, and four officers to each gate. Charlie takes it morning and evening, while the others are at gun drill. All, nearly, are obliged to learn the gun drill from some Artillery Sergeant, to be ready if wanted. Our entrenchments, they say, are now very strong; we have several mortars, and two 18-pounders are placed at the entrance to the Cawnpore road. A reconnoitering party went out, and returned in the evening, saying there was not an enemy to be seen for miles round. This evening there was a fire seen in Cantonments, but it was accidental; however, they got an alarm in the night, as several Sowars were seen riding about; they also had an alarm at the Muchee Bawun. Captain C— — woke them up and said a party of the enemy were coming, but it ended in nothing.

Saturday, June 20th. Charlie came about half-past 7, and stayed nearly an hour. After breakfast Dr. P—— read "Guy Mannering" to us while we worked. I cut out and made a flannel shirt for Charlie, as I could get no durzie. We are forbidden now to go over to the Residency or the Begum Kotee, as there is small-pox in both. In the former Mrs. B—— has it, and one of Mrs. B——'s children. Mrs. B—— is removed into a tent, in all this heat! To-day a letter came from General W—— at Cawnpore, saying they still held out, but had provisions and ammunition for only one fortnight longer; that no reinforcements had reached them, but that their greatest enemy was the sun: more had died from sunstroke than had been killed by the enemy, and that their greatest consolation was that they were keeping the enemy from us. It is most distressing that we cannot send them any troops; but if even we could spare them, they could never get across the river at Cawnpore, for the enemy have both sides of it; firing, both musketry and artillery, was heard all day in the district. The landowners are fighting amongst themselves, to get back what was taken from them at the annexation. A fire was seen burning in the district all night.

Sunday, June 21st. Rose at daybreak as usual, and went into the garden for a breath of air; the heat at night is fearful. Charlie came in at half-past 7; he is looking better, he is not so exposed at the Muchee Bawun as he would be here; still, he has never taken off his clothes at night since he went on guard the week I left Cantonments; he is always sleeping at some gate or other: but he looks better than could be expected, and says his appetite has returned. We had service in the drawing-room—Mr. H—— performed it—for the church is filled with stores. In the evening, service was performed in Mr. G——'s garden, the two Padres reading and preaching under a tree; but the heat was so great I could not go. In the night we had the first fall of rain, and welcomed it accordingly.

Monday, June 22nd. Rose at daybreak and took the air in the verandah, as it was raining. However, it cleared in time for Charlie to pay me his visit. The day passed without a word of news, or any alarm. Dr. P—— went on with "Guy Mannering," and I worked at Charlie's flannel shirt. Miss N—— came over in the evening and said Sir M—— J—— and his two sisters were hourly expected. I had a note from Mrs. R——, at the Begum Kotee; her baby is very ill with dysentery, and she said the room was so filled with ladies and children with fever that when the poor little thing wanted to sleep it could not. She ended the note by saying she felt her child's illness and her anxiety for her husband's safety were almost too much for her.

Tuesday, June 23rd. Charlie came as usual; he has been present at two hangings: the day passed without news, either good or bad.

Wednesday, June 24th. Charlie came late; I was quite proud to show him his flannel shirt, and sent it for him to try on. I went down with Mrs. F—— to her godown (store-room) and saw all her stores in case of a siege—rice and flour—all in large earthen jars, that reminded one of the jars the forty thieves were put into, in "Ali Baba." Certain news reached us to-day that the enemy are closing round us; there are eight regiments with six guns at Nawab-Gunge, twenty miles from here; it is said they intend coming here, and encamping in the Dil Koosha.

Thursday, June 25th. Another day without a word of news, good or bad; even gentlemen begin to croak.

Friday, June 26th. The first news in the morning was good. Mrs. B—— heard of the safety of her husband. I went in, as usual, at 7, to take my bath, that I might be ready for Charlie; and Miss S—— came running in with the good news, sent by Sir H. Lawrence, that Delhi had fallen on the 13th—that Futteyghur, Mynpoorie, and Etawah were quiet—the telegraph open to Delhi—and the dawk to within twenty miles of Cawnpore.[6] Glorious news! a salute was fired. Charlie came, but would not stay; he wanted to take back the news to the Muchee Bawun, and have the salute fired before ours. We cannot be too thankful! the insurgents at the best, are cowards; and this news will quite quell all spirit in them. Charlie had been to gun-drill—all in the garrison have to learn it. The rest of the day passed as usual, Dr. P—— reading to us till 4 o'clock dinner; after that I generally lie down till 6 and then take the air in the Compound—at 8 they generally bring tea and ices, and then Mr. H—— reads prayers and we all go to our rooms.

Saturday, June 27th. It was little Bobby F——'s birthday; he was one year old. Charlie came at a quarter to 8, and told us Capt. H——'s murderer had been captured at Allyghur; also that it was reported the 12th N.I. had mutinied at Jhansi, and killed every one of their officers; a letter came from Col. W——, at Cawnpore, with a list of the killed—about half their number; he said that their sufferings had surpassed anything ever written in history, and that their greatest enemy had been the sun; many ladies and children had died from it: but now they had dug underground places and put the women and children in. Brigadier Jack and his brother had both died from sunstrokes. In the course of the day came a pencilled letter from a Mr. M—— at Cawnpore, to his father, Col. M——, here, saying that they were treating with the enemy; this threw us all into consternation, for we thought General W—— would have stood out to the last; however, it is said to be the Rajah of Bhitoor (the Nana), who has commenced the treating with them. A lac of rupees has been set on his head, if brought in within a week. I suppose he had heard of this and became frightened, for he offered General W—— to conduct them all down to Allahabad safely, if they would lay down their arms and give him a lac of rupees. This Rajah is a Mahratta, a notedly treacherous race, so that we were very glad to hear firing had commenced again at Cawnpore;[7] proof that, of course, Gen. Wheeler would not agree to such a treaty.

Sunday, June 28th. The rain had been pouring down all night, the first regular rain we had had; there had been nothing but a storm before, and now I was rather disappointed at its coming, for Charlie had agreed to come at half-past 5 and take me to Mr. I——s' house to get some things out of a wardrobe we have placed there, and he was to be back in time for service at 7 at the Muchee Bawun; however, he could not come, and we could not go to service here in the mess-house on account of the rain. About 2 we got a slight alarm, hearing that two guns, some Europeans,

[6] This was a *ruse* to deceive the enemy and keep them off a little longer—which we were not told at the time.

[7] This must have been the firing into the boats instead. Poor creatures! we little thought it was the horrid massacre going on.

13th Sepoys, and 71st Sikhs, had been ordered off somewhere; however, it turned out that they had been sent to the King's palace for all the jewels. Two Nawabs were sent with them (I forgot to say we have five Nawabs prisoners in the Muchee Bawun), and they were made to understand that if there were the least disturbance they would be shot. Some fighting was expected, as there were armed men in the palace. Charlie came about 3, and stayed an hour. About 6, as we were going to church, we saw all the party returning, the carts filled with great boxes, and the golden throne, said to be worth a crore of rupees! Captain W—— told me some of the crowns were most elegant, the designs really beautiful, and also some of the necklaces, in one of which the diamonds are set in rays; one crown is silver set with amethysts. The King kept his own European jeweller, a man from H——'s in Calcutta. We set off walking to church, which was held in the Thug hospital belonging to the Thug goal; it is now the mess-house for all the infantry and cavalry officers. We had to enter by innumerable little arches of curious architecture, and up and down lots of steps and through two quadrangles, and then came in front of what appeared to be a Musjid,—the whole side open with beautiful arches,—they had begun service; rows of chairs had been placed for the congregation on either side of the mess-tables; the reading desk had been brought from the church. All round appeared to be little dark rooms, in which the officer's beds had been placed; also the large platform outside was filled with chairs, and beds were standing about in all directions. It was a most extraordinary scene; there was an immense congregation, and the whole place was filled with ladies and gentlemen. Mr. P—— read prayers, and Mr. H—— preached; the poor people at Cawnpore were prayed for; also Dr. S—— of the 32nd, who is very ill; and all in hospital, sick and wounded: and then those who had lost relations in these frightful massacres. It was a most imposing service, and one could not but feel thankful for having been so mercifully preserved. Some officers came in late, all booted and spurred,—I fancy from the party that had just brought in the jewels. We had a thunderstorm during service, and at the end were rather alarmed at hearing three guns fired, but it must have been in the district; they are fighting and quarrelling amongst themselves. It rained when we came out of church, and was very dark, so I and Miss S—— stumbled on the best way we could over the steps and uneven ground, hardly knowing which way to take; it was such a novelty walking to church in India, and especially under an umbrella. Soon after our return it poured down famously; we had tea and ices, and then Mr. H—— read prayers, and we retired for the night.

Monday, June 29th. Sir H. Lawrence and his Staff came while we were sitting in the garden, to take a survey of Dr. F——'s defences. Charlie came at 7, and I went with him to Mr. I——s' house, to my wardrobe. I could not recognise it for our old guard-house, where I had been so frequently with Charlie on city duty. All the buildings are thrown down round it; it is in the outer entrenchment. The Compound was filled with tents with Crannies and their wives; the day passed without alarm.

Tuesday, June 30th. I rose early, and found Dr.—— all booted and spurred for service. I then heard a detachment had been ordered off to meet the enemy, who were five miles off. Three hundred Europeans, nine guns, and an 8-inch howitzer, and 150 of the 13th N.I., &c., went out. I sat, as usual, in the garden, till 7, and then went in to bathe and dress, and be ready for Charlie. However, to my surprise, he never came, and I sent off a note to the Muchee Bawun asking the reason. While the servant was gone with it, some came flying back saying our troops had been surrounded by the mutineers, who were in great numbers, and that several of our officers had been killed. Just then, to my horror, came back the note I had sent with a message from Captain F—— that my husband had gone out with the detachment. I never shall forget that dreadful suspense as the news was brought in that Col. C——, Capt. S——, Mr. T——, and Mr. B——, of the 32nd were killed. The latter had always paid us a visit, mornings and evenings. At last came Dr. P——, saying they were sorely pressed by the enemy, but that he had seen my husband all right. Soon after came a Sepoy, sent by Charlie himself, to say he was all safe; and immediately after a 13th Sepoy, of his own accord, came to tell me he had seen Charlie coming in on a gun as he was very faint, and that Major B—— was wounded. I was frightened, thinking Charlie had got a sunstroke. He told me, afterwards, he had had a most narrow escape, as he was far back in the retreat. It had proved far different to the expectations of the morning, for the Native Artillerymen had proved faithless; and, the enemy being in far greater numbers than our spies had led us to expect, our little party was almost surrounded, and it was only a wonder any escaped to tell the tale. The sun also was so overpowering that many fell down from sheer faintness, without a wound, and were cut to pieces by the enemy, for few had any horses to return with. The officers had dismounted to fall in with their men, and the horses disappeared; either the enemy or the servants made away with them,—poor Charlie's dear old charger amongst the rest; the poor horse that was shot in the nose the night of the mutiny. It was a fearful morning, never to be forgotten, this affair of Chinhut! Another providential escape for dear Charlie, for which we cannot be sufficiently thankful! The siege now commenced, the enemy began firing on us as they followed the retreating party. Our gates were closed, we got a cup of tea and something for breakfast as best we could, sitting behind the walls to escape the balls; not that I fancy any of us had very much appetite. At last the balls came so thick that we were all ordered down into the Tye Khana (underground room), and kept there. Towards evening the firing slackened a little, and we sat in the portico to get a little air. There were twenty-four of us in the house—eleven ladies, six gentlemen and seven children. Captain W—— was the commandant of our garrison, which consisted of an officer and some twenty of the 32nd Queen's, with some Native Pensioners, and a mixed party of men to work the 18 and 9-pounder guns in the garden. At night we purposed sleeping in our own rooms, but Dr. F—— considered it not safe to do so; we therefore all stretched our bedding on the floor of the Tye Khana, putting the children in the centre for the benefit of the punkah. We took it by turns to watch for an hour.

Wednesday, July 1st.[8] We just managed to get to our rooms and dress, when the firing got very sharp—round shot and shell; already we began to distinguish the different sounds as they whizzed past: in the afternoon the enemy got into a building very near and fired away at us till evening, when they slackened again.

[8] Miss Palmer had her leg taken off by a round shot in the Residency this day, and only survived it twenty-four hours.

I got a note from dear Charlie, saying he was all right again I felt so thankful. Shortly after came Capt. W— —, to whom I read it; he begged me to copy it for Sir Henry as there was more news in it than in any that had been received from the Muchee Bawun; he also said they had paid 100 rupees for getting one carried there. I copied it, and he told me that I should soon see Charlie; and we heard the garrison of the Muchee Bawun had been ordered to come in that night at half-past 12, evacuating the fort as silently as possible, and blowing it up. We all expected they would have to fight every inch of the way in, and were in great anxiety in consequence; however, we went to bed, and I even slept, when about half-past 12 we were awoke by the most horrible explosion. It shattered every bit of glass in the house! There were four doors to our Tye Khana, half glass, and the concussion covered us with the glass, and shook one of the doors off its hinges. I believe all of us thought our last hour was come; each started up with a kind of groan, for we had been expecting the enemy were mining, as we had fancied we had each night heard strokes of a pickaxe, about half a dozen at a time, and then a stoppage as if they feared to make too much noise: the gentlemen had been down to listen and heard it distinctly, so that when the explosion came, I certainly expected to go up into the air; and the inexpressible relief it was to hear Dr. F— —, at the head of the stairs, calling out "It is all right! The whole party are in safe, and the Muchee Bawun blown up!" No wonder the explosion was so terrific, there were upwards of 20,000 lbs. of powder, besides a vast quantity of musket ammunition!

Thursday, July 2nd. The attack on the Bailey Guard Gate and our Compound was tremendous, and while we were at breakfast we were all inexpressibly shocked and grieved to hear poor Sir Henry had been mortally wounded; a shell from the very 8-inch howitzer the enemy had taken from us at Chinhut, had burst in his room in the Residency, and given him a fearful wound in his hip! He was brought over into our verandah, and Mr. H— — administered the Sacrament to him. Sir Henry then sent for several whom he fancied he had spoken harshly to in their duty, and begged their forgiveness, and many shed tears to think the good old man would so soon be taken from us. Our only earthly hope in this crisis! Sir Henry then appointed Major B— — his successor. The firing was fearful; the enemy must have discovered from some spies that Sir Henry was at our house, for the attack on the gate was fearful. We all gave ourselves up for lost, for we did not then know the cowards they were, and we expected every moment they would be over our garden wall; there was no escape for us, if they were once in the garden! We asked Mr. H— — to read prayers, and I believe every one of us prepared for the worst; the shots were now coming so thick into the verandah where Sir Henry was lying, that several officers were wounded, and he was obliged to be removed into the drawing-room. We gave out an immense quantity of rag to the poor soldiers, as they passed up and down from the roof of the house wounded. Towards evening the fire slackened, but we were not allowed to leave the Tye Khana. At night Mr. H— — came and read prayers again, and then we (ladies and children) lay down on the floor without undressing.

Friday, July 3rd. When we awoke we found all the servants had deserted excepting my Kitmagar and Mrs. B— —'s, and one or two Ayahs. The F— —'s had not one servant left, so we were obliged to get up and act as servants ourselves, and do everything, excepting the cooking, even to washing plates and dishes; and perhaps it was a good thing, for it kept us from dwelling on our misery. Dear Charlie came to see me in the afternoon, and brought a jug of milk for the poor children. I was glad to hear he had had a good luncheon, for the day before when he came he said he had had nothing for some days but dal (peas) and rice; we happened to be at dinner, and I gave him a piece of meat, but he seemed too much done up to eat it, and actually carried it away in a piece of paper to some other gentleman who could get none. No arrangements have been made for messing at present, and no one can tell where to get anything.

Saturday, July 4th. Firing had been going on all night, and it continued all day, but we were so engaged in kitchen duties we scarcely noticed it. Poor Sir Henry died in the morning; he had been in great agony from his wound! He was buried with the rest at night, but even he did not have a separate grave; each corpse is sewn up in its own bedding, and those who have died during the day are put into the same grave at night.

Sunday, July 5th. The firing was incessant, and after breakfast Mr. H—— arranged all our duties, for up to this time they had been rather unequally performed; after that we had service in the Tye Khana, and the Holy Sacrament was administered. I so wished dear Charlie could have been present, it seemed so solemn and yet so comforting while the firing was going on around us!—nothing else occurred worth noting.

Monday, July 6th. The insurgents filled J——s' house, and kept firing into our Compound; we fired a number of shrapnell into the house, without dislodging them. We fancied they must be getting short of ammunition, for they fired all sorts of strange missiles—such as nails, pieces of ramrod, &c.

Tuesday, July 7th. Charlie came, after breakfast, and told me that a sortie was to be made into J——s' house; this was done between 1 and 2 P.M.—two officers and some men of the 32nd and Mr. G—— and some of our Sikhs—a hole was made through the wall of the Brigade Mess, opposite J——s' house, an 18-pounder firing down our lane all the time to distract the enemy's attention. A rush was then made, and every Native in the house killed—numbering some thirty or forty. In the afternoon we had the first really heavy fall of rain, and the enemy's fire slackened in consequence. Poor Captain F—— this night had one leg taken off, and the other shattered, by a round shot, while sitting on the roof of the Brigade Mess! Mr. H—— saw him after the amputation had taken place, and said he was very composed. Mr. O—— died from his wound received at the Redan battery.

Wednesday, July 8th. Poor Mr. P—— was hit in the body by a musket shot; fortunately, the ball made a circuit round the body, instead of touching any vital part: he received the wound in the hospital. The firing was very sharp. I felt quite knocked up, after my morning duties. Charlie came, after dinner, and sat about an hour; he then went over to the hospital to see poor Captain F——. He found him insensible and very restless, and the doctors said he was not going on well; about 9 o'clock he died. He and Mr. O——, and two others, were buried in the same grave; the funerals are always at night, as the fire then slackens a little. Sometimes, Mr. P—— and Mr. H—— have had to dig the graves themselves! Soon after we lay down for the night, we were aroused by an alarm; it was false, and had been caused by a soldier dreaming: but, towards the morning, we were alarmed again by the enemy making an attack on our gate. We all got up and prepared, in case we had to run to the Begum Kotee, for there had been a hole dug in the wall opposite one of our doors for us to escape by in case the enemy should pass the gate.

Thursday, July 9th. I rose and made the early tea for the whole party as Mrs. A—— was ill, and while engaged in it an order came down for bottles of hot water, Mr. D—— being taken with cholera; after breakfast he appeared better, but it did not last. About noon Mr. H—— administered the Sacrament to him, and at 1 o'clock he died. Mrs. D—— seemed wonderfully calm. After making tea in the evening I went and lay down on my bedding in the Tye Khana, feeling tired out, and fell so fast asleep, that they all came down and had prayers without my knowing anything about it.

Friday, July 10th. We were ordered to sit upstairs as much as possible, as the Tye Khana and Go-downs were considered unhealthy; fortunately, the firing was so slack, that we could sit at the front door. It was quite delightful to have a little cessation from the constant noise. Mrs. D—— joined us, and seemed quite calm and cheerful. Charlie brought over six bottles of mustard, as we had very little and it was in great demand in cases of cholera; in the afternoon he came and chatted with me. Mr. H—— had only one funeral this evening.

Saturday, July 11th. There had been an alarm in the night, but I had heard nothing of it. I rose and made the early tea; and while carrying a cup to Mrs. F——, slipped down some steps and sprained my ancle: it became so painful that Dr. P—— recommended my fomenting it with hot water, and laying it up—so I was unfortunately *hors de combat*. Charlie sold poor Capt. F——s' property, and made 500 rupees of a box of second-hand clothes, such a great demand was there for them; he afterwards brought me a box of his papers and rings, which I locked up for his poor sister, in case I should ever be able to give it to her. Very slack firing all day; the enemy occasionally fired pieces of wood shaped liked nine-pins, and bound with iron. There was a report that the Nana was this day coming to join the rebels. There were five funerals this evening.

Sunday, July 12th. We had slept in the dining-room for the first time—but the mosquitoes were fearful—as the punkah was too heavy to be of any good. About half-past 10, Charlie came and stayed to prayers; at 12 Dr. F—— made us all again dine in the Tye Khana, as the dinner upstairs brought such swarms of flies. In the evening the ladies sat under the portico and sang very prettily; Capt. W—— joining them just as they had sung one verse of the evening hymn: the enemy commenced firing so sharply that there was a call to arms, and the gentlemen all rushed off to their posts. The attack was first on Mr. G——s' house, and then came round to ours; we went to bed, but the firing was so loud and the mosquitoes so lively that we slept but little; in fact, we all wished ourselves down in the Tye Khana again.

Monday, July 13th. Rose, feeling wretched. My face is becoming covered with boils, but hardly any one is without them now. The firing still very sharp; a European soldier was wounded in the corner of our verandah. The enemy were said to be again in J— —s' house; a Native was shot dead, coming from the Begum Kotee to our kitchen: altogether, eight were hit in our Compound during the day. Charlie could not come till the evening, and then stayed only a few minutes. Mrs. T— — very ill, with the small-pox, at the Begum Kotee.

Tuesday, July 14th. Dear J— —'s birthday. I had slept soundly, though the firing had been very sharp all night. The 17th N.I. were seen with their colours amongst the rebels; there were all kinds of reports of relief—none true! Charlie came over about dinner time, and sat some time, but I could not offer him any: I drank J— —'s health in sherry. An attack was expected at night, and all preparations were made; we ladies were sent down to the Tye Khana to sleep. The rebels had placed an 18-pounder in position for our house; however, the ammunition for the gun was blown up, and we passed a quiet night, with the exception of a skirmish with the punkah coolies.

Wednesday, July 15th. Charlie came soon after breakfast, and told me the narrow escape he had had, from the careless firing of a 9-pounder by a sergeant who had been instructed by an artillery officer to fire shrapnell into J— —s' house; he fired one into Capt. C— —'s quarters, which Charlie had only a minute before vacated; he had been dressing on the very spot where the shrapnell burst. There was very little firing during the day, but Lieut. L— — was shot on the roof of Mr. G— —s' house; Capt. F— — came for Dr. F— —; they could not find the ball, but fancied it had touched the spine, as all the lower part of the body was paralysed. Our party sat in the verandah, singing songs and glees. It made me feel quite melancholy, for the round shots were whizzing overhead, and no one could tell but that the next might bring death with it!

Thursday, July 16th. We heard that our troops had had a fight with the insurgents at Futtehpore, who had come from Cawnpore to meet them, and that we had taken four guns. No one knows if this be true, but it is possible, and that our troops are waiting there for reinforcements. Mrs. T— — died of small-pox. The heat and flies were dreadful; in the evening Mr. H— — had five funerals, one, poor Mrs. T— —. He said he had had a most narrow escape; going to the churchyard, a shot struck the ground directly between the two dhoolies carried in front of him, and covered them with earth! That night I rebelled against watching; we had had quite a fight about it during the day.

Friday, July 17th. The enemy had an 18-pounder in position to fire on an angle of our house. Mrs. S— —'s eldest child died of cholera. Dear Charlie paid me his daily visit. The firing was rather slack; the heat during the day was so intense, that the soldiers were allowed to lie down in the drawing-room. Mr. H— — had three funerals this night;—Lieut. A— —, of the Artillery and Captain B— —, were both wounded by a mortar that the former was superintending the loading of. Lieut. B— —, Artillery, was wounded yesterday. About 11 P.M. we were aroused by a very sharp firing,—an attempt made again at the Bailey Guard Gate, but was unsuccessful; still I got up and prepared for a rush to the top of the house, as they say that is our safest place if the enemy get in; the gentlemen can defend us up there.

Saturday, July 18th. I will write exactly my employment this day to show how each day is passed. I arose a little before 6, and made tea for all the party; then, with Mrs. A——'s assistance, gave out the rations for the day—ottah, rice, sugar, sago, arrowroot, &c., &c. While doing this a 6-pound shot came through the verandah above, broke down some plaster and bricks, and fell at our feet; Mrs. B—— and some children had a very narrow escape; they were sitting in the verandah at the time, but no one was hurt. I then rushed at the Bheestie (the water-carrier), who was passing, and made him fill a tin can with water for me, which I forthwith "lugged" upstairs and bathed and dressed; it was about half-past 8 when I was ready, so I went to the front door to get a breath of air; at 9 down again to make tea for the breakfast, which consisted of a small piece of roast mutton, chupattees, rice, and jam. I then worked on some of Charlie's garments till nearly dinner time—4 P.M.—when I felt very poorly, but it passed off.

Sunday, July 19th. The firing was very sharp; there had been an attack during the night. Early in the morning two round shots came into the long room through the drawing-room, and yesterday while the ladies were sitting in the long room a 9-pound shot came in through the drawing-room and slanted through a side door—breaking down the door-post and covering several of them with dust. Charlie came in, in time for prayers, which Mr. H—— read at 12 in the entrance hall; we had been kept down in the Tye Khana till then: by dinner time I became very ill. Charlie had given me a piece of ration biscuit, so I had that with a glass of port wine, instead of dinner. This afternoon an 18-pounder came into the drawing-room; we were all sent down to the Tye Khana in a great hurry. It was after dinner this day that Captain W—— gave us the particulars of the Cawnpore massacre. He said it was Thursday, June 25th, when they began to treat; the Nana required that they should leave everything—arms, ammunition, &c.—and he would provide them boats; some lady in a dhoolie was carried over to the Nana—it is thought to have been Lady W——. On Friday lots of hackeries were sent down to the entrenchments to convey the party to the boats, but were returned, and on Saturday a lot of elephants were sent instead and the party mounted them; the sick, and ladies who could not travel this way, were sent in dhoolies, and the whole party was escorted by the Nana's force to a Ghaut about a mile from the entrenchments, where the boats were waiting. However, it was discovered that there were neither cars nor ropes to the boats, or boatmen; nevertheless, they were told to get in and drop down the stream; and two boats filled and got ahead of the others: the remaining eight were loading when a battery, masked behind some trees, opened fire on them, and the Sepoys rushed down and bayonetted the women and children—selecting fifteen or eighteen of the young ladies and taking them off to their camp! The two boats that had gone ahead were first fired into from the opposite bank of the river and sunk. At this juncture, they say, some of the 56th N.I. rushed to their rescue and a few escaped. I had been so ill in the morning that I had been obliged to have Dr. F—— to attend me,—and I was better towards evening, when the pain came on so violently I fancied I had cholera coming on. Dr. F—— gave me another dose of opium, but I was very ill all night and fainted away; they called Dr.

F—— to me, and he dosed me again and ordered a mustard poultice, I went up and lay down in Mrs. H——'s room—the only safe one upstairs.

Monday, July 20th. Towards morning the round shot began flying about thickly—two 18-pounders came into Mr. H——'s room while he was dressing; they came in high, and covered him with a cloud of dust: the bricks and mortar fell thick around him, but he escaped unhurt. Soon the attack became tremendous all around us: round shot flying in all directions; musketry on the roof of our house incessant. Strange to say, I never winced or closed my ears; however, I and Miss S——, who was kindly fanning me, decided we had better go down to the Tye Khana. Breakfast, however, all were too much engaged to come to. The attack lasted more than four hours; and they say, at the least, we were surrounded by 4,000; six of their guns were pointed at our house. About half-past 12, Dr. F—— called down to us that it was all right; and one by one the gentlemen came down to breakfast. They said the enemy had been beaten back, with great slaughter: one 32nd Sergeant shot fourteen of them, one had seen twenty killed here, another, thirty there. They opened the attack this day by springing a mine at the Redan Battery, but without harm to us. I continued very faint and weak throughout the day. While dinner was going on, about 5 o'clock, Charlie came over; I was so thankful to see him safe. One more providential escape he has had, and I could not feel sufficiently thankful: a bullet had entered his helmet at the side, gone out at the top, carrying the ventilator with it! He and his Sikhs are in a large house—Mr. O——'s kutcherry—and in a very small verandah, that they occupied during the attack, twenty-two round shots had come in. Charlie said they had attacked with the spirit of Europeans. Some Mussulmen Sowars, carrying a green standard, had tried to cross the stockade, close to his post; the leaders of the party were all killed, and the flag left in the brushwood. At this crisis a plucky man rushed up, and although his right arm was broken by a musket shot, he contrived to extricate it, and carry it off with his left. After that, an attack was made at the same point, by Sepoys, with muskets and bayonets, but also unsuccessfully. Another account Charlie gave of Mr. L——, commanding at our old guard-house—now I——s' post; they had the hardest work to keep it. Mr. L—— considers, at that part alone, 100 of the enemy were killed; so that all agree their loss must have been very great, whereas we had only two killed, and very few wounded: amongst the latter, Mr. E——, of the 32nd, at the Redan, and Mr. H——, 7th L.C. The 13th, at the Bailey Guard, behaved splendidly. This day, Mr. P—— died of cholera; his wound had been progressing nicely, when he was seized with cholera. Towards night, the firing had almost ceased. Mrs. B—— fancied her child had cholera, so we were kept awake the greater part of the night.

Tuesday, July 21st. I rose early, feeling better; while sitting at the door for air, Major B—— called in and chatted with us. Charlie came at breakfast to see how I was, and again at 1 o'clock, bringing me a saucepan of soup and a bottle of port wine to enable me to get up my strength again. Just after he left, the enemy made an attack, principally on Mr. G——s' house, and word was brought that Major B—— had been shot through the head on the roof of the house, and Dr. D—— wounded; the times are awful! Major B—— is, indeed, a loss; a tremendous attack was expected at night, but it passed off quietly; probably, on account of the heavy fall of rain we had. The siege has lasted, now, more than three weeks.

Wednesday, July 22nd. I made the early tea and breakfast; hardly any firing going on. Charlie came over and read some of my journal; after he left, he sent me over a saucepan of soup, and one of his ration biscuits. About 1 o'clock, Capt. E—— came running over from the G——s' for Dr. F——, as Mrs. D—— had been shot through the head as she was sitting in a bedroom just off the G——s' dining-room; her death was instantaneous. In the evening Mr. H—— had nine funerals.

Thursday, July 23rd. The first news in the morning was, that a Native Pensioner had come in from Cawnpore, with tidings that a large body of Europeans were at Cawnpore, and that they had crossed ten guns; they had had three fights with the Nana, and had burnt his house. Every one believes this; and we may expect them by the first proximo. It is glorious news, indeed! The Pensioner was sent off again, with a letter, and only one rupee (as he himself requested); but, if he brings an answer, he is to have 500 rupees, and a double pension for life. The man's name was Ungud. I now have to wash my own clothes, and this morning had a scrimmage for water,—Mrs. H——'s Ayah having had the impertinence to run off with my can of water, after I had had the trouble of bringing it upstairs. Firing, slack to-day; it is supposed many of the enemy have gone to meet our reinforcements. To-day, we spoilt the bridge of boats over the Goomtee, by firing round shot at it. The night was quiet.

Friday, July 24th. A grand scrimmage about the goats and milk for the children. The reinforcements said to be fourteen coss off. A round shot took off a portion of the roof of our house; but, the enemy's fire was generally slacker: a number of them are evidently gone off to meet our troops. Last night, as I was making tea in the store-room, the largest Bandycoot rat ran through that I ever saw, the size of a little pig. At night the Tye Khana was so disagreeable that we were obliged to burn camphor and paper in it.

Saturday, July 25th. My morning duties were rather heavy, having a large number of clothes to wash; and I have always to take up all the water I require, and carry it down again when done—labour that I thought I never could have been equal to, especially in this country. Charlie sent me one of his flannel shirts to mend; the front of it was torn to pieces. He had lent it to an officer of the 48th, who had none, and who, while wearing it, had had a most narrow escape. A round shot had come in and covered him with bricks, which had torn the shirt in the way stated; but he was uninjured. Charlie paid me his daily visit; he had been to Mr. P——'s sale. I told him how badly off poor Mrs. K—— was at the Begum Kotee, no one either to get or cook her rations for her. The day before yesterday her only food had been a few chupattees, and a cup of tea without milk or sugar. The enemy are shelling to-day. They sent one into the Dawk office; it made a hole through the roof, and, falling on the table, smashed it; but luckily, not bursting, it did no other harm. Some of Mrs. P——'s things came round for sale, and I bought a silk dress for twenty-six rupees, as I have lost every one of my own. Mr. T—— came with the order books to-day; it is the first time I have seen him since the meeting in Cantonments. Mr. A—— also came in the afternoon; both seemed pleased to see me again.

Sunday, July 26th. A letter arrived from the Quartermaster-General of the relieving force, saying that two-thirds of the force had crossed the Ganges, and would soon come to our relief; that they had quite demolished the Nana's force, and that they were strong enough to bear down all opposition. Glorious news! The Brigadier sent down an order for all officers to be more watchful than ever, and not to leave their posts. Charlie has to ask leave to come down and see me for half an hour. An attack is expected, as a last attempt from the enemy. Lieutenant L— —, of the Artillery, was shot through the head at the Cawnpore battery. He had just stepped aside to escape a pool of water, and was shot from a loop-hole. Mr. H— — was sent for to the G— —s' to administer the Sacrament to Mrs. G— —, who was dying of cholera; he returned, and we had service in the entrance-hall: in the evening it was held at the Brigade Mess. The enemy was discovered mining, to-day, towards the Cawnpore battery; so we commenced counter-mining: our people could hear the enemy working a little above them. A luckily-thrown shell of ours fell on top of their mine, and broke it in.

Monday, July 27th. There has been a sharp attack during the night, and Lieut. S— —, 7th L.C., was accidentally shot by one of the Europeans. Charlie came in for half an hour, soon after breakfast; he had a boil on his knee: he said our mine was progressing well—twenty-seven feet dug. Dr. P— — was very busy all the morning, getting his galvanic battery ready to blow up J— —s' house; he has had fever for the last two days. No news from the relieving force, though they said they should send a letter; it is supposed that all the approaches to the city are strictly watched. Charlie said that during the night a plan had been sent out of the entrance to Lucknow, by the Dil Koosha, as it is considered a more practicable route than the regular Cawnpore road. Firing was very slack throughout the day. Mr. H— — had two funerals.

Tuesday, July 28th. My morning duties, including washing clothes, very heavy. No news from the relieving force; firing slack. We left off the Cawnpore battery mine—as the enemy had stopped theirs—and commenced one in the Sikh square, where we found they had also commenced. In the evening our people managed to dig direct into theirs, which we destroyed with a small charge of powder. Col. H— —, who has been laid up with a carbuncle all the siege, was much worse to-night. While we were at prayers this evening, there were several volleys of musketry, so there was a call to arms, and Capt. W— — and the gentlemen rushed off to their post. Nothing, however, followed. Col. H— — died during the night; he has been in a small tent, in the garden, all through the siege.

Wednesday, July 29th. I was awoke by a mouse running over my neck, scratching me with its horrid little feet. Still no news! After breakfast I took Miss H— —'s duties for her; as, poor girl, she was not in spirits for it. Charlie paid me his half-hour's visit. I am so thankful each day to see him once more. After dinner, just as we came upstairs, guns were heard firing from the Martinière, and upon the top of the house smoke could be seen from two batteries; a regular royal salute was fired—twenty-one guns. All became excited in the greatest degree, considering it was our relieving force; but we were doomed to disappointment. No one knows what it was for; but there is a report that it was in honour of a boy who has been placed on the throne by the soldiery. An attack expected at night; but all was quiet.

Thursday, July 30th. Nothing of importance to-day; no news of the reinforcements. I felt very disheartened, in consequence. Two officers of the 71st came on Col. H— —'s committee of adjustment; they told us many wounded men had been seen brought into the city.

Friday, July 31st. Another most disheartening day; no news!

Saturday, August 1st. Firing slack; no news!

Sunday, August 2nd. No news again! Mr. H— —, 7th L.C., died to-day. The relieving force ought to have been in three days ago. God grant it may come to our assistance shortly! The poor children feel the want of fresh air and proper food sadly; but, still, we have much to be thankful for; for, we have, as yet, endured no hardships, and my dear husband has so far been spared to me.

Monday, August 3rd. Still no news! Firing, during the night, sharp. The enemy threw several shells, some of which exploded in the Begum Kotee; but, as yet, without injury to any one. Dear Charlie came and gladdened my heart. About sunset the shelling became very sharp again; one burst over Dr. P— —'s head, in the air, as he was going into Mr. G— —s'. About 200 of the enemy's cavalry were seen moving, which caused a little excitement, by no means unpleasing to us in our present inactive condition. The future is a perfect blank to us; we are not able to give even a surmise as to what our fate may be: but, we have made up our minds never to give in, but to blow up all in the entrenchments sooner.

Tuesday, August 4th. Another day without news. Firing sharp, during the night. Our only consolation is, that, no news is good news; for, if any reverse happened to our reinforcements, the enemy would quickly let us hear of it, and be back upon us immediately. A fine young man was shot to-day, at the 9-pounder, in our garden; he was shot through the lungs—he has left a wife and four children. Charlie came for his half-hour's visit, my only gleam of sunshine in the gloomy day. I had an enormous rat in my bedding when I unrolled it in the Tye Khana for the night.

Wednesday, August 5th. No news whatever; but very few of the enemy to be seen round us. While Charlie was with me to-day, it came in to heavy rain, so that I got more than my half-hour's chat; and sent him home in my blanket shawl, tied in a knot on his head, and hanging down all round like a cloak. Some of the enemy's regiments of cavalry and infantry were seen to parade in front of the Redan, and then go off to the Cawnpore road. Very little firing during the night.

Thursday, August 6th. Another night without news! Poor Mr. S— —, of the 32nd, had his arm broken in three places by a 24-pound shot, and his side hurt so badly that they fear he will not recover. All are to vacate the Residency to-day, as it is so unsafe.

Friday, August 7th, We were cheered by the news that a Sepoy of the 1st Oude Irregulars, who had been sent out by the Brigadier, had returned; he had lost the letter from the relieving force, but had been in their camp, and seen General

H——. He said they had four European regiments and one Sikh one; and that one European regiment had a curious baja (music) played in front of them—meaning the bagpipes: that our force had had a fight with the enemy, the first march out of Cawnpore, and taken eighteen guns. A little further on they had had a fight with villagers, who had decamped, leaving five more guns in their hands; and then our troops, hearing the Nana was collecting a force again in their rear, returned to Cawnpore. However, the Nana took fright, and was off and away; so they took in fresh supplies, and were coming on again. He also said Shereef O'Dowlah was the head of the rebels in the district. There were 200 cavalry with our force, principally volunteers and officers who had lost their regiments. About 3 P.M. the Sepoy came to see Mr. C——, and we heard all his tale. Whilst we were sitting in the long verandah room after dinner, there was a call to arms, and the gentlemen went off to their posts; and I went off to fetch the things I should require at night, for I knew if there were an attack I should not be allowed to go into the room where I dressed. A few rounds from the guns were fired, and the supposed attack subsided.

Saturday, August 8th. Mr. H—— went over to baptize Mrs. K——'s child, as it was dying. Mrs. B—— and her child are also very ill; indeed, so are all those in that room at the Begum Kotee. Dr. M——, 41st N.I., and Lieut. B——, both died of cholera this day.

Sunday, August 9th. Mrs. B—— taken ill during the night, and at 8 P.M. a fine boy made his appearance. I thought of poor Mrs. D——, who, we were told, was confined in the open at Cawnpore, in the rear of a gun; she and the child were both massacred afterwards. Mr. S——, and Mrs. K——'s baby, both died to-day. Mrs. H—— rather angry at being turned out of her room to give place to the new baby. Mrs. D——, who is expecting her confinement, had a fainting fit; altogether a nice commotion. In addition to a sharp attack, with heavy firing from some of the guns close to us, a 9-pound shot came into Mrs. C——'s room, and just as we were talking of coming up to sleep in the dining-room again, two shots came in quite hot, which settled the matter.

Monday, August 10th. A Sikh came in during the night; he said he had been made prisoner at Chinhut: however, he is thought to be a spy, and is confined. His account of our reinforcements agree with what we have previously heard. About 11 A.M., Lieut. B——, A.D.C., came round to warn all the garrison to be on the alert, as some regiments had been seen, with their colours flying, marching from Cantonments. As they crossed the Cawnpore battery, we fired on them, and the attack then commenced; the firing was very sharp: shells, shrapnell, round shot, gingalls, and musketry. I now can distinguish each plainly. Of course, I always feel very anxious, after an attack, before the list of casualties comes round. To-day two Europeans were killed, and five wounded—wonderfully few, considering the firing was incessant till about 2 P.M. Two of the enemies' mines were exploded, but without injury to us. About 5, just as we were coming up from dinner, dear Charlie made his appearance, with some clothes for me; but would not stop, as he said he had just seen another little army coming up to the attack; it consisted of two regiments of infantry, some cavalry, and five guns: he hurried off, and the firing commenced. I much troubled on his account, for his house has lately been so battered by round shot, it must be very unsafe; however, Dr. F—— told me he had seen him all right. One of the mines sprung in the morning, destroying one of the rooms where the Martinière boys are, but without injuring any one: however, it sent one of the heavy timbers of the stockade on to the roof of the Brigade Mess (an upper storeyed house), much to the alarm of the ladies residing there. We heard that Mrs. O——, of the 48th N.I., had had a little boy during the night. Just as we were going to bed, another attack commenced; the night was very dark, but we were providentially preserved through all.

Tuesday, August 11th. All quiet. I rose early, as my morning duties are generally very heavy. After breakfast Charlie came; I felt so thankful to see him safe once more. He told me the enemy, thirty in number, got into the Compound next us, last night, but were driven out by hand grenades, &c. During the forenoon, we heard a rumbling noise, and, on inquiry, found that one wing of the Residency had fallen, and buried six men; two were dug out alive, but only one survived it. The rest could not be got out till late in the day. Charlie told me that the day before, when the enemy's mine exploded at Sago's, two Europeans were blown out into the road, with their muskets in their hands, but being uninjured, they jumped up and ran though his gateway, and through the stockade to their posts again. From this one may imagine our defences were but slight.

Wednesday, August 12th. There had been incessant firing all night. No news, whatever, has been brought in! Charlie came and gladdened my heart; but I must say my own hope of relief was sinking.

Thursday, August 13th. Native reports that our forces are near, and firing has been heard distinctly in the district from the Redan battery for two hours—so hope revives. We countermined and blew up a mine of the enemy's at Sago's. It was well done, and it is supposed numbers perished, including the miners themselves, who were heard at their work just before; several of the enemy rushed down to dig out comrades, but of them four were shot.

Friday, August 14th. A sweeper came in this morning. Charlie caught him near the hospital, and carried him to Captain C——'s. He told them a great deal about the enemy; but, of course, nothing could be relied on. He said that the Native report was that our force was at Bushire Gunge. Mrs. F—— was very ill, and removed to Mrs. D——'s room.

Saturday, August 15th. No news from without! We had our beds brought into the dining-room, and for the first time during the siege we were to sleep on charpoys (bedsteads). The last three nights in the Tye Khana I have slept on chairs, to escape the rats; for the last night I slept on the floor I felt my bedding heaved up, and a large black rat ran from under it. This is the third time we have tried to sleep in the dining-room; twice we have been driven out by shot. This afternoon a shrapnell burst on the roof, wounding two Native Pensioners and a European sentry; an 18-pound shot also came in.

Sunday, August 16th. The first news we heard was, that a letter had been brought in from the relieving force; but, to our disappointment, it proved to be an old one—the man having been imprisoned. After his release he had returned to Cawnpore to get further news, but found, with the exception of a small force entrenched on this side, that they had re-crossed the river—the Nana having collected a fresh force. He also said that numbers of troops were on their way up the country, and that when a sufficient party had arrived—which would be about the 20th—General H—— would again advance. In the afternoon a shrapnell burst in Mrs. F——'s verandah, close to her present bedroom; some of the pieces passed over her and Mrs. B——, going through the venetians, and setting fire to the chicks; she was brought out and placed in Mrs. B——'s room with the new baby. I fought against sleeping in the dining-room, as I thought it dangerous; but, being in the minority, I was obliged to give in.

Monday, August 17th. We passed the night without an accident, though the roof was hit by round shots. Mrs. F——'s little boy Bobby very ill; he looks a perfect skeleton: as for Mrs. D——'s youngest boy, you can count his bones; they are only just covered with skin. It is a terrible time for poor children; they pine for fresh air.

Tuesday, August 18th. We were awoke by an explosion of one of the enemy's mines in the Sikh Square; no one knew they were mining there: it buried six half-caste drummers and a Sepoy, and blew two officers into the Square, who escaped with slight bruises. This made a great breach in our defences, and the enemy might have come in easily if they had only had a little pluck. Three of the leaders tried to induce a party to make a rush, but failed; and, two of them being shot, the affair ended. There was a great firing of round shot and shell, but only one of our men was killed and none wounded. Bobby had been very ill all night, and Miss S—— sitting up with him; so, at 5, I got up and relieved her, and after breakfast I had to complete my wash of clothes. No news of our reinforcements! During the day a sortie was made, and young J——'s house was blown up: they found eleven men in it, whom they bayonetted; they also blew up a lot of houses in the neighbourhood. A shell had gone through the roof of one of them, and underneath there was a large pool of blood. Two of the enemy's mines were destroyed with their own powder, and one by pouring a quantity of water down it; so they are paid off for the morning. At sunset Mrs. F—— was brought out on her bed into the verandah for air. At night, as we were all sitting under the portico, we heard a peculiar cry, three times repeated, and thought it might be a signal; sure enough it was. Then there was a cry at once, "Stand to your arms!" followed immediately by a great discharge of musketry and great guns. All the posts had been warned to be on the alert, but the attack did not last long. About 3 in the morning, Mrs. D——'s youngest child died.

Wednesday, August 19th. No news! After breakfast Mrs. D—'s poor baby was sewed up by Mrs.—— in a clean table cloth, she having first dressed it in a clean night-dress and lace cap, and crossed its little arms on its breast; the little thing was carried to the hospital to await its burial, at night. The day passed as usual.

Thursday, August 20th. No news again! The night had been very quiet. As I was sitting at the front door at work, a European was shot, at the gun in our garden, right through the head. Mr. C—— was wounded. I had a very bad boil on my hand, for which I made an ottah poultice; our dinner this day was stewed beef, dal and rice, and chupattees. We were told, before going to bed, that J——s' large house was to be blown up at daybreak.

Friday, August 21st. We had a most disturbed night. There was an attack about 12, and I heard, "Turn out! turn out!" called from the gentlemen's room; and, being half asleep and half awake, out I and Mrs. A—— rushed from our bed over two other ladies in our haste; and, much to our amusement, several of them scolded us famously for making such a rush. We thought, however, we had a right to leave our bed when we chose, especially as we had about the most dangerous corner of the room; this amused us so much, that we lay down again in a fit of laughter. I heard almost every hour strike during the night. At daybreak, J——s' house was blown up, but it did not shake us so much as we expected.

Saturday, August 22nd. I rose very early, as I had so much to do. I was engaged till noon. While Mr. C—— was in the gentlemen's bath-room, a round shot came in and covered him with bricks and mortar, but did him no injury. This morning, a sortie with about 100 men was made; they blew up some houses, spiked three guns, and killed many Natives, with the loss of one killed and several wounded; two, they fear, mortally. The rest of the day passed quietly. Our dinner to-day was roast mutton, but very little of it, so we opened a tin of salmon, and Mrs. N——, a woman who has charge of Mrs. B——'s children, made us a roly-pudding of ottah and suet—to us a perfect luxury.

Sunday, August 23rd. I always try to have some clean garments ready to put on on Sunday, as one way of recognizing the day. There was service at the Brigade Mess at noon, and in our house at 3 P.M.; Mrs. F—— and Mrs. B—— came over to it, and lay on couches. Col. P—— brought over Mrs. P——, Mrs. B——, and Mrs. L——, three young newly-made widows; Mr. C. D—— and Charlie also came. Mr. H—— administered the Sacrament; it was placed on a small round table, covered with a white cloth: it was an affecting meeting—so many had lost friends! Poor Mrs. P—— was sobbing all the time. Mrs. L—— had lost both husband and child!

Monday, August 24th. I rose with a distracting headache, from the constant firing of the heavy guns during the night; the enemy sent three round shots into our house, and the guns in our Compound returned the fire. Mrs. C—— was ill with erysipelas. A Kitmagar came into the entrenchment to-day, but was put in confinement on suspicion of his being a spy. Mr. G—— came about 4 P.M. for Dr. F—— and Dr. P—— to go to the post office with their amputating instruments and chloroform, as Mr. M'C——, C.E., had been shot in the arm; however, they did not consider amputation necessary: a sergeant and private were shot at Sago's. I could hardly recognise Mr. G——, he looked so much older with a beard and the effects of his late fever.

Tuesday, August 25th. A sharp attack on the Bailey Guard Gate kept us awake the first part of the night. I got up and dressed as I usually do, though it is perfectly useless; we have no safe place to go to. Mrs. B——'s child kept us awake the latter part. No news of our reinforcements: very little firing to-day, Mr. and Mrs. H—— came in the afternoon, both so nicely dressed; one could hardly fancy the siege was going on.

Wednesday, August 26th. Dearest mother's birthday. We had a wretched night with Mrs. B— —'s children and the firing; I actually lay till 7. I then went down for my cup of tea without milk or sugar, or rather mug, for I use Charlie's silver mug now; cups have become so scarce. Dear Charlie sent me a beautiful bouquet of roses, myrtle, and tuberoses; it is such a treat to have a sight of lovely flowers again! Oh! the longing one has to be out in the fresh air again! wandering in fields or gardens. But the useless dreams only do one harm. We have the stern realities of life before us; so to return to them. I went and acted as my own laundress; to-day our rations are reduced: gentlemen get twelve instead of fifteen ounces of meat, and we six instead of twelve; with rather less dal. A sentry was shot through the leg in our verandah during the night, and Dr. F— — was hit by a spent ball. After breakfast I mended a pair of Charlie's unmentionables with a piece of Mrs. H— —'s habit, presented for the purpose: he came for a little chat, but a note from the Brigadier called him away. A little milk-punch is "doled" out to us every day about 1 o'clock, and I drank dear mamma's health in mine. I sat at the door till dinner time, 4 o'clock, making flannel garments for myself, having luckily taken a new piece of flannel into the entrenchments with me. After dinner the invalids came out and took the air on their couches at the door; at 7, I made tea for all, then sat at the door till half-past 8, when we had prayers and went to bed; and I had a good night's rest, though the children were rather squally. Lieut. W— — 32nd Queen's, killed by a round shot to-day at Mr. G— —'s.

Thursday, August 27th. No news. The enemy fired an immense number of shot and shells; one soldier wounded in our drawing-room verandah, but it was his own fault; they are forbidden to go there, as it is dangerous. Sir H. Lawrence's stores were sold to-day, and fetched enormous prices: a bottle of honey, forty-two rupees and upwards; a dozen of brandy, 107 rupees; a ham, seventy rupees; two tins of soup, fifty-five rupees; a small bottle of pearl barley, sixteen rupees; twenty bottles of sherry, 110 rupees. People seemed to bid recklessly, Charlie said; they were to be paid for on the first issue of pay, which many, I believe, think they will never live to receive. Charlie bought, instead, a pair of soldier's high-lows, for eight rupees, from a Sergeant—quite a catch; and far more useful than truffled larks, &c.

Friday, August 28th. No news again! This is very trying—the siege has lasted now more than two months. Every one agrees that the only plan is to blow ourselves up, if the reinforcements do not come in time. I rose very early, as Mrs. A— — was ill; and having a great deal of work to do, I did not sit down till 12 o'clock. I have a chance of having some things washed by a dhobee, but at the exorbitant charge of twenty-five rupees per 100! more than eight times the usual charge. We expected an attack to-night, as the Mohurrum and Mussulman fast is just over; it did not, however, take place.

Saturday, August 29th. Rose and I did all Mrs. A— —'s work again. A Pensioner came in during the night, with a letter, direct from Gen. H— —, dated August 24th, saying he was waiting for more troops, and could not come to our relief under twenty-four days; he added, that Sir C— — C— — had arrived in Calcutta, as Commander-in-Chief, and was sending up troops as quickly as possible; that

Lucknow would be his first care, and also begging us, on no account, to treat with the enemy, but rather to die at our posts. The man who brought the letter said, when he was in General H— —'s camp, a man had come from Delhi, who told him we had an immense force before Delhi; partly composed of Bombay troops. The day passed quietly; only the usual firing; no attack.

Sunday, August 30th. When we got up, we discovered our two remaining Kitmagars had fled. Many Half-castes and Natives left the entrenchments last night, having heard our relief was not to take place for some time. Mrs. H— — and I had to boil the kettles, in addition to our morning duties; Manuel, a Madras servant Dr. F— — has just picked up, lighting the fires for us. We all had to help in preparing breakfast and dinner, and washing up. We had no service till late in the evening, as Mr. H— — had one at the Brigade Mess, another at Mr. G— —s', and a third at the Hospital. I got perfectly worn out, with running up and down stairs; but I am thankful to say I am in excellent health, and thoroughly enjoy my meals.

Monday, August 31st. We were awoke at daybreak, by Mrs. D— — being taken ill. I ran down sharp to light the fire and boil the kettles—the former by far the most difficult operation—I am very stupid at it, and before it was completed, down came Mrs. C— —, saying the baby was born. It was a most expeditious affair; they had hardly time to get her into her own room. Mrs. C— — finished boiling the kettle, while I prepared the early tea-things. I worked really very hard this morning in the kitchen store-rooms, and it is anything but a joke this hot weather to have to stand before the fire fanning it to make the kettle boil. I was quite tired out before all was completed; but I am a perfect wonder to myself. I never thought I was capable of such fatigue, or was half so accomplished as I find I am. Mrs. B— — and her baby were turned out of the invalid room for Mrs. D— — and her's. Great scrimmage with another Mrs. B— — about her European servant being allowed to cook for us; we carried our point. The cooking establishment, now, consists of Mrs. N— —, slightly assisted by Manuel and two little boys from the Martinière school; the latter are useful in the washing-up department. The enemy tolerably quiet to-day, no shells till 9 P.M., when there was rather a sharp attack, but not of long duration.

Tuesday, September 1st. Went to my regular work, and discovered the two Martinière boys were to be taken from us; so there was another grand scrimmage about washing up plates and dishes. The enemy brought a gun to bear on the Bailey Guard Gate again. (I forgot to say that on the 30th ultimo, our miners discovered a mine of the enemy's close to them; so Mr. F— — sat nearly the whole day in the mine, pistol in hand, waiting for them to pick into it; they, however, stopped, so we broke into theirs and blew up the gallery. Lieut. B— —, Artillery, was also shot in the chest, while sitting in the portico of the dawk office talking to Charlie). This day, Tuesday, two Artillerymen were shot in the dawk office compound, while standing by the 18-pounder; the ball, a round shot, ricocheted from the hospital. One had some property in his box, and though the officer sent for it immediately, the box was missing; however, it was recovered before the thief, a brother gunner, had had time to open it. The looting now is something dreadful; many of the Crown Jewels have been stolen, and a bottle of brandy will now purchase a handful of precious stones. Charlie told me he had seen a handful of pearls, one of them very large, and many of them the size of peas, which had been purchased for twenty rupees.

Wednesday, September 2nd. The sexton's wife came to help. Mrs. N— —. The enemy were discovered mining, close to the Financial garrison; so we countermined, and blew them up. Several of the enemy were seen rushing to the spot, to try and recover their blown-up comrades. A sad occurrence took place today! Lieut. B— —, Assistant Engineer, was shot by one of our own sentries while searching some ground just outside our works, in the dusk of the evening, to see if there were any mining going on; he was taken to the hospital in great agony, having been shot through the stomach. Mr. H— — took his poor wife to him; he died during the night.

Thursday, September 3rd. Nothing particular occurred.

Friday, September 4th. A day without news, and tolerably quiet. Poor Major B— —, who, while trying to get a shot at the enemy, on top of the Brigade Mess, exposed himself unnecessarily, was shot through the lungs, and survived it only about ten minutes; those who went up to fetch his body, had to crawl on their hands and knees. At night his own Sepoys carried him to his grave.

Saturday, September 5th. Much firing in the early morning. The 13th Sepoys made a battery for an 18-pounder, at the Treasury, with which Lieut. A— — made some good shots at the clock tower. The firing ceased a little, when all at once we felt a mine spring, and immediately an attack was made by the enemy; the firing then on both sides was incessant. In the midst of it we felt another explode, which we thought was our own; but it was not: we did however, spring one during the day, and Mr. F— —, and a 32nd man, not having had sufficient warning, were blown up, but not hurt. In this day's attack 10,000 men were said to be around us; still they did not get in, and we had only two Natives killed, and two Europeans wounded; one losing an arm, and the other a leg. It was only Providence who could have saved us with so little loss: we have great cause for thankfulness! Our Sepoys are delighted at having a gun at their guard. They say "We load it, and Aikeen Sahib fires it!" They are behaving splendidly. At night there was another attack, and the firing lasted about an hour. A row between the Padre and a lady,—clerical victorious, and the lady going off into hysterics. The rest of the gentlemen were out digging, to repair the defences at the Baillie Guard Gate.

Sunday, September 6th. Several explosions during the morning, as our people were blowing down walls. At half-past 5 we had service, and Mrs. B— —'s baby was christened, in a little silver font, and she herself churched. In the night we had another attack. The musketry was incessant, and the great gun shook the house again. Mrs. A— — and I sat up till it subsided; the mortars close to us began shelling them: the attack began to subside, and all settled down again.

Monday, Sept. 7th. Nothing particular occurred.

Tuesday, September 8th. Captain S— —, of the Artillery, died at 4 A.M.; he had been severely wounded at Chinhut, and never recovered it. No news from without!

Wednesday, September 9th. I was awoke by our great guns firing at the clock tower; at 10 we sprung a mine at the Cawnpore battery. Mr. A— — came and had a long chat. Dear Charlie came while we were at dinner, and was much amused at my enormous appetite. We had a dreadful night with Mrs. B— —'s youngest child, and poor little Bobby.

Thursday, September 10th. Tremendous firing at the mosque, by the clock tower. Two or three 18-pounders at it, and shelling also, as the enemy have lately occupied it with their sharpshooters, much to our annoyance. All quiet afterwards. About 2,000 men were seen to leave the City towards Cawnpore. In the evening, and at night, a number of hackeries followed, it is supposed, with their baggage. Prices are rising. Twenty rupees given for 2 lbs of sugar, and one rupee per leaf for tobacco.

Friday, September 11th. A tolerably quiet day, but discoveries made of "Light Infantry" where they ought not to be. Mrs. B— —'s baby very ill; it has large ulcers all over its body, and inflammation in the throat. We destroyed two of the enemy's mines to day, and in one of them men were heard to screech.

Saturday, September 12th. A noise was heard during the night—a humming, as of Sepoys turning out of their Lines for a march; and many were seen in the morning dressed in marching order; they say the Nana is here, and is sending off his baggage to Fyzabad. Mrs. B— —'s child very ill; mortification must have taken place: I could not stay in the room. Mrs. H— —'s bearer wounded.

Sunday, September 13th. Capt. M— —, 32nd, who commanded our guard, died of cholera; he was taken at half-past 11 last night. We had service at half-past 2, and Charlie came. Mrs. B— —'s baby died in the early morning; it changed immediately. A spy was caught in the entrenchments, who said it was reported outside that several of our regiments had crossed the Ganges at Cawnpore. A very quiet day.

Monday, September 14th. Another spy caught, who said the Nana was still here, and that there is to be a grand attack to-morrow. Capt. F— — killed by a round shot, while examining the defences at Mr. G— —s'; he was an indefatigable engineer, and consequently a great loss.

Tuesday, September 15th. Some sharp firing, but no attack. Lieut. F— —, who was sick in hospital, and slightly delirious, walked over the parapet of the portico; he died shortly after. In the afternoon a large round shot came in through the top of the house, passing through two walls and cutting a belt hanging there clean in two; it then rolled along the roof, without doing any damage.

Wednesday, September 16th. Sharp firing. At 6 A.M. a shell came into the Treasury Guard, wounding two 13th Sepoys severely and one slightly. We have two people in the garrison who were in the siege of Jellalabad—one, the celebrated Dr. B— —, who says, that was a gentlemanly business compared with this; the other, a queer, dilapidated, old half-caste, a corporal at Charlie's post, who, some say, was a spy there, and he says, that was a trifle to our siege. Charlie had four round shot into his house this morning in a quarter of an hour; he has certainly been most mercifully preserved. The rest of the day was quiet. In the evening some horrible smells came from the buried animals, &c., that we could not sit at the door as usual to take the air.

Thursday, September 17th. No news! We are beginning to get very anxious again. They say our beef will only last till the 10th proximo. The enemy are throwing up another battery, which will sweep the whole garrison excepting our house; we try, with our shells, to prevent them working at it. We had a quarter of mutton to-day for dinner, and a suet pudding afterwards, with some of Capt. W——'s patent sauce, Mr. C—— having begged about a quarter of a pound of sugar for it; this made twenty people as merry as formerly a dinner with the Governor-General would have done. Our allowance of beverage for twenty people is two bottles of indifferent champagne and one of claret and two pints of beer for two sick ladies. Yesterday, Mr. D—— gave a bottle of brandy and a bottle of sherry for twenty-five cheerots. Mr. H—— found a soldier of the 32nd, with his head knocked off with a round shot, lying in the churchyard, when he went to his funerals; so he buried him at once. Queer things happen sometimes, as I could testify about a Roman Catholic and a Protestant who had to be buried the same night; on arrival at the burial ground it was doubtful which was which, but it was summarily settled by an officer present.

Friday, September 18th. We had a slight attack in the night; while dressing this morning a bullet came into the outer room with such force that it struck off one side of the frame of a picture, leaving the glass whole. My labours increase every morning. An eclipse of the sun was visible between 9 and 11; a tolerably quiet day. As we were sitting talking in the evening, I ventured to say I thought we had never passed an hour—day or night—since the siege began, without some firing; I was immediately laughed at, and told *not five minutes* even! If this ever reaches my dear ones at home, they will wonder when I tell them that my bed is not fifty yards from the 18-pounder in our garden—there is only one room between us—and yet I lie as quietly when it goes off as if I had been used to it all my life: eighty days of siege life does wonders! This is getting a most anxious time; if our relief does not come within the next twenty days we must look for no hope in this world, and we have heard nothing of them yet; but God is above all, and nothing happens by chance! I commit all to Him, and if He spares me and my beloved husband to meet our dear ones in our own beloved country, I will indeed be thankful; but it is a fearful suspense!

Saturday, September 19th. A tolerably quiet day; but I became very ill.

Sunday, September 20th. Still very poorly. We had service and communion at our house. Charlie came to see me twice, as I was so unwell.

Monday September 21st. No news. Dr. F—— ordered me to keep my bed; there I was in the dining room, all open to the public, the gentlemen passing and repassing the door: there was no help for it, however, as it was the only room we could have a punkah in, Charlie came and sat with me and got Dr. F—— to write a certificate for me to have a little sugar and sugee from the Commissariat, as it was kept for the sick; he also brought me a bottle of port wine from the Brigade Mess; but Dr. F—— said I must not take it till I was better.

Tuesday, September 22nd. Still obliged to keep my bed; no news.

Wednesday, September 23rd. Still in bed. No news during the day; but at 11 at night, came Col. P— — cheering us all with the news that a letter had just come in, brought by Ungud, the same faithful spy—saying that our reinforcement crossed the river at Cawnpore, on the 19th, had a fight at Enown on the 20th, another at Bushire Gunge on the 21st; and were hastening on to us. The heavy rain we are having must detain them, but it is glorious news indeed!

Thursday, September 24th. Guns distinctly heard, about ten or twelve miles off, firing for a length of time, so the troops must be nearer than was expected. I cannot describe our feelings at our present hope of relief, all are in the height of expectation. Being a little better, Dr. F— — allowed me to get up. The guns of our force heard approaching nearer and nearer. Oh! the thankfulness one feels at the certainty of relief now! I think, if I were stronger, I should be more joyous. The smoke of the guns seen from the top of the Residency! Oh joy! they say they are only four or five miles off! but they have to fight their way in! Fifteen thousand went out to meet them; but, from the heavy rain, took no guns with them. We had a very disturbed night; the rebels made two furious attacks, and came up again about 5 A.M., but were soon silenced.

Friday, September 25th. The guns of our reinforcements commenced again, and one gun kept firing for an immense time. They say they are on this side of the Char Bagh, about four miles from us, and the smoke and flash of the cannon may be seen from the top of the Residency—musketry heard distinctly. If they have sent any messenger on to us, none has arrived; it is a most exciting time—far beyond description. The first feeling is gratitude to God for deliverance from the horrors of famine, which was staring us in the face, and, apparently, not very far distant. I lay in bed till after breakfast, as the disturbed night had not done me much good; but I enjoyed two sugee biscuits dear Charlie sent me the night before for my chota hazree, with my tea sweetened with sugar, which I had not tasted for many weeks. These sugee biscuits the ladies in this house are buying at five rupees the pound. My longing now is to get a Dhobee and an Ayah; for I feel so weak and helpless, with not a single person to help me, and so unable to do anything for myself. Some kind friend always brings me my meals, &c.; but I feel that they all have as much as they can accomplish, without doing my work as well. About 12 we heard that the rebels had broken up the bridge near the Char Bagh, so we decided our troops could not be in for some time; however, all of a sudden, I heard our soldiers shout out, "They are coming!" their caps could be seen, and we found they had crossed by the Martinière bridge. Immediately a fierce firing commenced, and they said the rebels were flying off to the Fyzabad road. We commenced shelling them: there was a tremendous day's firing, notwithstanding, and the troops had a fearful day's work. About 5 P.M. we heard cheering, and, immediately, we saw the troops rushing in, the 78th Highlanders foremost, and our house, being near the gate, the Compound was instantly filled. A Mr. W— —, an officer heading the Highlanders, rushed up and shook hands with us ladies all round, and then threw himself into a chair quite exhausted, and, in an instant, the whole place was filled with them; it was as much as we could do to supply them with water. It was by far the most exciting scene I ever witnessed. The Piper sprang on a chair, and he and Mrs. A—— fraternised. He asked her where she came from, and when she answered from Edinburgh, he shouted out "So do I, from the Castle Hill," and immediately sent word round that there was a lady from Edinburgh amongst us, and then gave another tune on his bagpipes. The Ferozepore Sikh Regiment also accompanied them, and some of the Madras Fusiliers. The confusion and excitement was beyond all description; they lost some hundreds coming through the City. General O—— then came in; he had been wounded slightly in the arm. Dr. F—— dressed his wound. He and his staff took up their quarters in our house. Strange to say, no one had brought any provisions, though they confessed they expected to find us in a worse condition than they did. They said they had hurried on, because they had seen five ladies and four gentlemen on their way, attempting to join them, and feared they were some of our garrison; the poor creatures had all been cut up by the rebels. The news they brought in from all parts was far more horrible than we expected. At Jhansi the brutes had burnt the poor children before their poor mothers' eyes, and then killed the wives, and then the husbands. At Cawnpore they found only two living beings and a heap of dead women and children, being those who escaped the massacre at the boats. They say the place where the murders were committed was a most heart-rending sight; not a soldier left it with a dry eye. We heard also of the B——s' of our regiment having been murdered at Hissar. Every one was trying to get news of his friends; scarcely one but heard bad news. A detachment, with some guns, was left at Allum Bagh in charge of the baggage and stores. The men and officers had only just what they wore. During the night, I heard the soldiers conversing in the drawing-room, where they lay, and one man said they had made a high caste Brahmin sweep out the go-down, where the massacre took place. I was obliged to go and lie down early; but several of the ladies made tea in the Tye Khana, for any officers who would partake of it, and numbers went down. We had neither milk nor sugar to give them.

Saturday, September 26th. Several parties went out to take the guns on the palace side of us; portions of the force are also occupying the Fureed Bucksh, the Teree Kotee, and jail formerly occupied by the enemy. Tremendous firing all day. I not seeing my husband became very uneasy, and found he had been sent out on duty at the Fureed Bucksh. I passed a wretched night!

Sunday, September 27th. The first thing I heard on awaking was, that a Sikh was waiting from my husband, asking me for tea, and saying that Charlie had had no food since yesterday morning—so I sent him a bottle of tea and some ottah for chupatties. I was only too thankful to find him alive and well. He afterwards sent me in a cut glass jug he had plundered, and then came himself, but quite lame from the boils on his knee. A party went out led by Mr. A—— to take some guns, but unfortunately did not succeed. Charlie came again in the afternoon, but appeared quite done up; he is now on the sick list. Miss N—— came over, and several other ladies were walking about—quite a novelty. I walked down nearly to the garden gate, the first time since Chinhut, June 30th. We had service in the Tye Khana, and Mrs. D——'s baby was christened.

Monday, September 28th. I got up, feeling wretchedly weak. This was to be a day of rest for the troops; however, we rather expected an attack, as it was the Dusserah—a very warlike festival. Numbers were seen crossing the bridges, but it passed off quietly. About 2 P.M. came a messenger from Allum Bagh with news from Delhi, saying our flag was flying on the Cashmere Gate, and that we were in possession of five gates, the Church, Magazine, and Mr. Skinner's house, the College, and had fixed a battery at each gate of the palace—where the king was—who had determined to fight it out. Of course, a day or two must finish it! The messenger also brought a letter from the detachment at Allum Bagh, saying they were all right there, but that the enemy had broken up the bridges between us and them. Dear Charlie came at dusk, as he is on the sick list, and brought me some of his books. Numbers of the "big dogs" assembled in our house to-day, planning with General Outram; I fancy the attack to-morrow.

Tuesday, September 29th. A detachment of 800 men went out into the City at daybreak, and we were continually hearing explosions from the blowing up of houses; one shook us like an earthquake; they took nine guns and did their work well. Although we can scarcely call this a relief, seeing we have to feed the new troops on our own scant rations, and are reduced in consequence; still they are able to make sorties now, and have discovered three mines under the Redan, that would have done us awful damage—we cannot therefore be too thankful that they are come in. A piece of shell to-day passed through Mrs. F——'s little room, and struck the wall by the gentlemen's dressing-room.

Wednesday, September 30th. A letter in from Allum Bagh, saying they were all right there, and had not been attacked; great consultations going on in the General's room with all the "big dogs," and such sending off of despatches. Charlie came after dinner; his knee was very bad. In the night the cavalry were all started for Allum Bagh, but the firing was so sharp that they were obliged to return.

Thursday, October 1st. No news. They were trying to batter down some houses, near the iron bridge, all the morning, and making a tremendous noise. Two parties went out: one to take the guns about the Cawnpore Battery, and the Sikhs to take a bazaar. They were out all day, going on slowly, but surely. At night, the Sikhs had got as far as the Painted Magazine, at the corner of the Karse Bazaar; and the other party had got into some houses close to the Cawnpore road, where they meant to remain the night. The General and "big dogs" were out all day, at the top of the Brigade Mess, watching their movements. Dear Charlie came quite lame—the doctors say we must all get scurvy, living on the same food, and so long without vegetables; he brought me some china and a beautiful punch-bowl—his own looting.

Friday, October 2nd. Dear J—— and L——'s wedding-day. Where shall we spend our own? Nothing done this day; but a rumour went about that all the Native troops were to be sent out to the Allum Bagh: of course, their officers must go with them. If true, I think it is very cruel to separate us, after enduring our three months' misery together.

Saturday, October 3rd. They say our troops are still gaining ground in the City. Several of the enemy's guns were blown up to-day. Charlie brought me some more china.

Sunday, October 4th. We came out in clean and new dresses, that we had kept for the relief. Mrs. H— — and Mrs. B— — went to service at the Brigade Mess. We had service in our own house, at 8 P.M.: several gentlemen came; Charlie amongst them. After dinner, I went over to his garrison, with Dr. P— —, and was perfectly thunderstruck to see it such a mass of ruins. Not a portion, on either side of it, that is not riddled with round shot and bullets; the verandah all knocked down—it is impossible to tell there had been any; there are large pieces of masonry lying about. From the outside, you would not think the house at all habitable; and even the centre room, that Charlie occupies, has immense holes in the walls, made by round shot. He took me on the roof, as the enemy are too far off to be dangerous now: I could hardly tell which were the houses that had been occupied by the enemy, and which by us; there was merely a bamboo stockade between us, and the marvel is they never got in. I was told, "just down there, a 9-pounder was firing into us night and day, and a little further off a smaller one." Charlie's post was fired into sharply, day and night; and I could only feel thankful for his wonderful preservation through it all. I little thought the fire he had been always exposed to. I enjoyed a cup of tea with him, of course without milk or sugar; but it was such happiness to be alone with him again. He gave me a beautiful manuscript, worked in small green and white beads, on pink and gold paper—Dr. F— — said no doubt done by the ladies of the Court. At night, a letter came in from Allum Bagh, saying they were all right, but surrounded by the enemy's cavalry.

Monday, October 5th. The day passed as usual. After dinner we had such heavy rain, it prevented my going to Charlie's post; he paid me a visit instead.

Tuesday, October 6th. We had a grand attack; the enemy actually got into the Fureed Bucksh, but were killed in great numbers. Our troops were drawn in a little, as it was not considered safe for them to be out so far. They had got as far as the Delhi Bank, on the Cawnpore road, but the enemy have it again now, and also Metaz and Dowlah house, which was said to be filled with jams and pickles, so that our visions of delicacies were doomed to be blighted.

Wednesday, October 7th. The anniversary of my arrival in Calcutta. An 18-pound shot came in. The guns are further off now, but I think more dangerous, for we never know their range now; and two or three round shots come into the house every day, on all sides. In the evening, General Outram came and sat with us, and while chatting a despatch came from Allum Bagh. These despatches are written on thin paper, and rolled up so small that they are put into a little piece of the quill of a pen. This brought good news—that 250 men had arrived at Allum Bagh, with two guns and fifty commissariat carts, and had met with no opposition on the road. The bridge at Bunnee was broken, but the river fordable.

Thursday, October 8th. I have resumed my labours, and the whole morning was taken up with receiving rations of ottah, rice, salt, &c., and seeing them weighed. Poor Mr. G— —, of our regiment, died to-day.

Friday, October 9th. I took possession of my go-down, at the request of several of our party, and had all the provisions put under my charge. Captain A.

B— — died. Dr. B— — brought the news, and went with Mr. H— — to his funeral. A letter came from Cawnpore in the evening, saying Delhi was entirely ours; but that several regiments of the enemy, with 18 guns, had escaped, and were coming to Lucknow: however, a large force of our troops were pursuing them, and hoped to intercept them before they could reach us.

Saturday, October 10th. A letter from Allum Bagh, saying they were all right. They are seven hundred strong, and have nine guns. They had sent out a foraging party, and brought in lots of provisions. We had a quiet day.

Sunday, October 11th. A busy day with me, for I had to take in the rations for all for three days. In rice, we were reduced to something less than 6 lbs. for all the party, for three days. Charlie came to service at 3. No news till night, when another letter came from Cawnpore, saying the Delhi column had fallen in with the Jhansi mutineers, killed 150 and dispersed the rest, at Bolundshuhur, on, I think, the 4th, and were coming on to relieve us, and might be expected the end of the month. We had two attacks during the night; the musketry sounded all round.

Monday, October 12th. Dr. F— — taken with fever. Three sales of deceased officers' property took place; Mr. Green's amongst them. Charlie said 260 of his small cheroots No. 3, fetched 500 rupees. I heard to-day an officer in our regiment had given a bottle of sherry for a cake of soap. No news!

Tuesday, October 13th. We had had a great deal of firing during the night. The day passed quietly. No news!

Wednesday, October 14th. Another day passed as usual. In the evening came a letter from Allum Bagh. All right there, but the servants were running away from not being able to get provisions. Reinforcements expected here about the 25th. A Sikh came in saying other Sikhs were anxious to come; he had deserted at the commencement of the siege. He was told they might occupy and keep a house just outside the entrenchments.

Thursday, October 15th. A quiet day, but all officers are ordered to remain at their posts till further orders, or until the Dewallee is over, as they say they intend to make a grand attack. The Sikh yesterday said they knew they could not take our position, but meant to starve us out, considering all the reinforcements that could come in time to save us had already arrived. In the evening came another letter from Cawnpore, and I understand the messenger brought a letter from Lady O— —, at Agra, in which she said they still drove out, and took the air as usual.

Friday, October 16th. All comforted by getting a grand breakfast of beefsteaks, a little rice, and dal and chupatties. During this morning Mr. D— —, of the 53rd N.I., who had survived the massacre at Cawnpore, called and gave us full particulars of the whole affair; poor Mrs. J— —, of the 53rd N.I. (she and I were brides together in Delhi), died in the entrenchments, and he was killed in the boats, but nothing was known about their children. At the commencement of their siege they had only 300 fighting men—soldiers, shopkeepers, and all included—and 400 women, and about 200 children. General W— — did not make the entrenchment at the magazine, because he had no idea that there was any ammunition in it; he thought it was filled with old tents, &c., whereas a great portion of the ammunition brought against us came from there, besides what was expended by the enemy at Cawnpore. This seems hardly credible in a General of Division, but I believe it is correct. Mr. D—— was in the only boat that got away; they pursued and fired at them, then the boat struck on a sandbank, and they took to the water, and their numbers were eventually reduced to four, who were sheltered by a small Rajah until General Havelock's force arrived at Cawnpore, when they joined it. He said, he had to swim and wade six and a half miles after he left the boat.

Saturday, October 17th. My busy day. We had had a slight attack during the night. Two letters came from Cawnpore, giving accounts of our reinforcements. They will not be here quite so soon as was expected. The 93rd are to be at Cawnpore on the 23rd instant, and the 23rd on the 2nd of November. Sir Colin Campbell is coming over here himself with the troops. I trust they will not delay it too long; for, famine is too horrible to contemplate. Our daily rations of meat are now 12 oz. for a man, 6 oz. for a woman, and 2 oz. for a child, and this is bone inclusive, which is sometimes nearly half; and we have had 9 lbs. (the ration for our party for one day) of which 5 lbs. was actually bone. Then seventeen of us (some choosing to have their rations separate) have 15 lbs. of unsifted flour for our chupatties, 6 lbs. of gram to be made into dal (this is private store food, generally given to horses), 1 lb. 12 oz. of rice, and a little salt. We generally make a stew of the meat and rice and a few chupatties, as it goes farther; but I think the gentlemen generally get up from table hungry. We have still a little tea, but neither sugar, milk, wine, nor beer; our beverage is toast and water, a large jug of which is always placed on the centre of the table; it is made of the old chuppatties, if any are left of the previous day. All horses under 150 rupees value were, by orders, destroyed at the river yesterday, as they were eating up the gram.

Sunday, October 18th. Charlie came at 3 P.M. to service, and was much amused to hear we were going to have a sparrow-curry for dinner. Dr. F—— had shot 150 sparrows for it; most pronounced it very delicious, but I could not be induced to try it. I agreed with Charlie to pay Mrs. B—— a visit, as I had not seen her since the Major's death; so I went with Dr. P—— to the Brigade Mess, and Charlie met me there. I also saw Mrs. P——, who looked very haggard and worn—worse than Mrs. B——. The ladies at the Brigade Mess are all living in dirty little rooms, in a large square; Mrs. P——'s had only one opening, serving as entrance door, window, and all. They say the rats are horrible; and I should think centipedes and scorpions also. At night we had a grand attack, principally at the Cawnpore battery, Mr. G——'s, and the Brigade Mess. The firing made more noise than ever I remember; the air being now so clear, as it is the commencement of the cold season, the guns reverberate tremendously.

Monday, October 19th. No news till the evening, when letters came in from Cawnpore, saying the Delhi force were within five miles of Cawnpore, but were fighting with Gwalior mutineers, and that the 93rd and 23rd Queen's were very near Cawnpore also.

Tuesday, October 20th. My busy day for rations. I also cut out a coat for Charlie's Sikh subadar, and was fully occupied all day.

Wednesday, October 21st. Our wedding day! so I must give full particulars of it. I rose at half-past 6, and had a cup of tea and chupattie and went to my store room and received and weighed the ottah brought in from grinding, and gave out the wheat for the next day; also our daily rations of ottah, rice, grain, onions, and salt; then acted as laundress to myself; at 10 breakfasted, then finished putting the subadar's coat together, cut out and made a black silk neck-tie for Charlie, and he sent me over a lot of rupees to keep for Mr. G——'s estate. I then read till dinner, which was composed of stewed meat, a little rice and dal, and a chupattie and toast and water. After dinner, Charlie came for me, as we were to spend the rest of the day together. I carried over a cup and saucer, teaspoon and wineglass, the subadar's coat, and a book I had borrowed for Charlie. I found he had got a pint bottle of champagne—his rations for four days at the brigade mess, as sherry and port were all finished. He, however, would have us finish it at the time, toasting our noble selves and our dear ones at home; he had made me with his own hands some sugee cakes with the remains of some sugee I had intended for him while ill. He had not been very successful; however, the will was good. He then went and begged a little milk from one that had that luxury, and I had been presented with a little sugar for the occasion, and having a little cocoa left of bygone days, I contrived to manufacture a very delicious cup, which Charlie pronounced capital, and we thought of the grand dinner we had eaten at the Barrackpore Hotel that night six years; it was a strange contrast to our half rations in a battered garret, but I don't think it made either of us discontented—only thankful that our lives had been so mercifully preserved through such awful scenes! No one can see the battered condition of Charlie's house—an outpost—without feeling that he has been almost miraculously preserved. He walked home with me about half-past 8, and I went to bed.

Thursday, October 22nd. While dressing this morning, firing was distinctly heard in the distance. No news in!

Friday, October 23rd. Distant firing heard again. About 3 in the morning, a messenger came in without letters; he had been obliged to put them down a well. He said the enemy had captured nine of our elephants at Allum Bagh. The day passed quietly.

Saturday, October 24th. No news! After dinner Charlie came, and I returned with him; and I had no sooner arrived than a 24-pounder shot came in! I took tea with him and afterwards came Captain W—— and they examined a Native who had come in. Captain W—— also came. I returned about 8. I always walk very quickly, both going and coming; but I cannot get over the imaginative sensation of having a bullet between my shoulders.

Sunday, October 25th. The General came and told us he expected the Madras column was close to Allum Bagh; he had received no letters, but a Native had come in. Charlie came to service at 3. The day passed quietly.

Monday, October 26th. Letters had come in, in the night, with capital news; the Delhi column had beaten the Mhow mutineers and taken all their guns, and were coming quickly to us, and that 6,000 troops would be at Cawnpore the 10th of next month and here about the 15th. Still they cut our rations down again—14 oz. of wheat a day for a man and no gram or dal for any one, and a smaller portion of rice, so that we can only have it once a day now. Just before breakfast, as I was sitting in the verandah, Col. Napier[9] came up and chatted with me; he had just been visiting the outposts, and said he had not till then had a full idea of what we must have suffered, and added, "I understand your husband has been acting nobly all through the siege." I scarcely thought till then he even knew my name amongst so many ladies. Col. Napier was on the General's staff. I, of course, said I was much gratified to hear such praise; but I went down to breakfast as happy as a queen, to think dear Charlie was duly appreciated, and to hear his praise from such high quarters. His position has been a most dangerous one—a very exposed outpost—as the walls will show. This was the day for the prize auctions—the property that had been collected from the palaces. I knew that Charlie was going, but had no idea that he intended purchasing; however, while I was in my room, Mrs. C—— came running to tell me he had arrived with a most beautiful Cashmere shawl for me. I ran out, and Charlie threw it into my arms; this seemed one of the bright days of the siege. He came over again for me after dinner, and I returned with him to tea, and just at the time a shell burst in the Compound below his house, but without damage.

Tuesday, October 27th. Letters had come in again during the night, saying the Delhi column was expected at Cawnpore on the 28th. Mr. G—— was mortally wounded at the new battery on the mound behind Mr. I——s' house. Dr. D—— was struck by a piece of shell, as he was walking down to the Ferard Bucksh.

Wednesday, October 28th. Letters came in again during the night, from Cawnpore, saying the Delhi column had arrived, and they had had three fights with the enemy—one near Agra, one at Mynpoorie, and one nearer Cawnpore,—and that they had routed them well and taken their guns; and that by the 7th proximo 2,500 of the troops coming up country would have arrived at Cawnpore; and that, altogether, we should be 8,000 strong. The day passed quietly. I went to tea with Charlie, and while there the enemy commenced a slight attack.

Thursday, October 29th. No news in! A very quiet day.

Friday, October 30th. No news! I went to tea with Charlie; while there a round shot came in and wounded one of the garrison by causing a brick to strike him.

Saturday, October 31st. After breakfast Charlie came and put up my mosquito curtains, as Mrs. A—— and I had the luxury of sleeping away from the party. We had Mrs. F——'s room to ourselves, Mrs. A—— being an invalid. I returned with Charlie and had a delightful morning. I altered a jacket for him; it is astonishing how clever this siege has made me in tailoring, &c. I returned about half-past 3. Everyone thinks it very dangerous my going to his house; but his room is tolerably safe—at all events, as safe for him as me, and it is delightful to have a nice chat together, for we know not how soon we may be parted.

Sunday, November 1st. Commencement of another month of the siege! Where will the 1st of December find us? It is coming to a crisis now. But the Almighty has

[9] Now Lord Napier of Magdala.

spared us through so much danger, I trust He will bring us out of it; my hope now is strong! We had a quiet day; no news!

Monday, November 2nd. The enemy threw several shells. I went, notwithstanding, to Charlie's quarters, and had a cosy evening with him. On my return, as were sitting in the verandah, a letter came from Allum Bagh, and the General, after reading it, said, he must tell the ladies the good news. The Commander-in-Chief was to be at Cawnpore this day, and that part of the force was already sent on to Allum Bagh, and that the rest remained to escort the Commander-in-Chief, who, it was conjectured, would push on to Lucknow immediately. The General said he did not like part of the force being sent to wait at Allum Bagh, as it would give the enemy the idea that they were afraid to enter Lucknow. The old gentleman then became very facetious, and asked if we would take the Commander-in-Chief into our mess in the Tye Khana, and other little jokes. I afterwards learnt that the arrival of the troops at Allum Bagh was to be signalled by three salvos of four guns each.

Tuesday, November 3rd. The enemy had been firing tremendously all night, and this day an attack was expected, so all were ordered to remain at their posts; Charlie, therefore, could not come to me. I got Capt. W—— to escort me over to his post, and spent a very pleasant morning with him; I making a cloth jacket. Charlie went with his men for a few minutes to help to put up the semaphore intended for the Residency to telegraph with Allum Bagh; the enemy sent a number of round shot and shell in, during the evening and night.

Wednesday, November 4th. After breakfast, I went over to Charlie's house, escorted by a Sikh whom he had sent. I must not forget to say that in my store-room I had a very advantageous deal with Mr. S——, 10 lbs. of green dal and 10 lbs. of wheat for 20 lbs. of rice, so that we can have a little rice with our breakfast now, as well as dinner. I made great progress with my cloth jacket, cut out of the surplus part of a habit; no news in! Mr. D—— had both his legs taken off by a round shot, while sketching in the Residency Compound.

Thursday, November 5th. Gunpowder plot. We had an attack during the night, and a great deal of firing, but it was quieter during the day, No news from without!

Friday, November 6th. A messenger had come in and told the General that Manu Sing had gone off with his men to Chinhut. I suppose he wishes to be neutral. I spent the morning with Charlie. A 24-pounder came in and wounded a poor woman by the bricks it dislodged. I completed my cloth jacket, and Charlie gave me some bloodstone buttons for it. In the evening, after Mrs. A—— and I were in bed, Mrs. H—— came in to tell us that a letter had come from Cawnpore, saying 5,000 Infantry, 800 Cavalry, and 36 guns, with 400 of the Naval Brigade, would be at Allum Bagh by the 10th at latest. Glorious news for us prisoners!

Sunday, November 8th. A quiet day—no news! Charlie came to prayers, and I went to tea with him.

Monday, November 9th. Another quiet day! I spent the morning with Charlie.

Tuesday, November 10th. A great deal of firing at Allum Bagh; several considered the four salvos that were fired the signal of the arrival of the troops, but others thought they were only signal guns. Mr. C— —, assistant to the Chief Commissioner, had gone out during the night to Allum Bagh, disguised as a Native, and during the morning the General sent word to his wife that his arrival had been signalled. At 8 P.M. a tar barrel was lighted at the top of the Residency, for some signal or other, and was answered from the Allum Bagh.

Wednesday, November 11th. There had been a good deal of firing during the night. No news in! A very unexciting day; they tried to work the semaphore, but from some mistake it did not answer.

Thursday, November 12th. I spent the morning with Charlie, arranging and packing our worldly goods; for, if the troops come in, we may be sent off at a moment's notice. We could see the semaphore working famously to-day for full three hours, and afterwards were told that Sir C— — C— — had arrived at Allum Bagh, Mr. C— — was all right there, and they did not intend commencing operations till Saturday the 14th—all glorious news! While I was with Charlie, there was a Native report that the troops were already coming in and the enemy flying, so several officers came to Charlie's to see from the roof of his house whether it was true; it turned out all false. After dinner, Mrs. B— — and Mr. C— — called, the latter I had not seen during the whole siege; he was looking better than I expected to see him, but his knee was much contracted from the wound he received in Cantonments the night of the mutiny. About 7 P.M. there appeared to be an attack commencing, but the firing did not last long—however, all officers are ordered to remain at their posts till the troops come in.

Friday, November 13th. I spent the whole morning packing the few worldly goods I have left, and the Oude china, for we may very probably be sent off at a moment's notice. After dinner, I went over to Charlie; we had a very quiet day. In the evening, a messenger came in from Allum Bagh but he had lost his despatch, so he was packed off to the Guard-house immediately; for, considering it had been telegraphed from Allum Bagh that the troops would move, without fail, the next morning, this letter might have been of infinite importance.

Saturday, November 14th. The troops moved from Allum Bagh. It was a very exciting day to most people; but somehow or other I felt very tranquil. I spent the morning with Charlie. The troops took possession of the Dil Koosha and Martinière, and by the evening our flag was waving over the latter building.

Sunday, November 15th. The General went out with his Staff at 10 A.M., but from some cause unknown to us, neither our troops made any sortie nor the reinforcements any advance. I paid Charlie a visit after dinner.

Monday, November 16th. A most exciting day. The troops moved from the Martinière at half-past 6; we heard the guns firing tremendously. I went over to Charlie about 11 A.M.; the roof of his house was crowded with spectators. They had just seen some of our Cavalry and Artillery take two of the enemy's guns, on the road to the Motee Mohul, and plant two of ours in their stead, drawn by grey horses; some of the Lancers were distinguished by their peculiar caps. Our own force, from entrenchments, moved out also from the Fureed Bucksh, and took the

Engine House and King's Stables, and all the buildings up to the Nullah. About half-past 12 I went on the roof (or rather stood at the head of the stairs, looking through a hole in the parapet, that had been made by a round shot), and saw the mines[10] sprung, and the batteries firing furiously behind the Chutter Munzel. It was a most extraordinary scene! shells were bursting in the air above them, —fired, I suppose by the enemy, —and every few minutes a new mine was sprung, sending up a thick yellow smoke and dust quite different from the smoke of the batteries. We saw one round shot strike a bungalow, on the banks of the river, and immediately some figures sprung up from the verandah and made off with their bundles of bedding. Many rockets were also fired, which set fire to several buildings, and then volumes of thick smoke and flame arose. At one time a mine was sprung, far out in the distance (conjectured to be some magazine of the enemy); very few were seen running away; every now and then, two or three would swim the river, having first stripped and tied their clothes on their heads. A few ran away in our direction, through Phillips' garden, so Charlie placed a rifleman to pick off any who might be seen flying in that direction. He would not allow more than fourteen on the roof of his house at one time; it was in such a battered condition, it was not safe to have more. It was doubtful even if the concussion from the mines might not shake it too much, so a Crannee and a Sikh were placed to keep too many from crowding up; and when some parties had been long enough, they were sent down, and others took their places. There was always a party of European soldiers waiting to go up: the house stands high, and commands the part of the city our troops are entering. I was quite sorry, when dinner-time came, and I was obliged to leave, for it was the most exciting scene I ever in my life witnessed. I little thought even when I "listed," that I should ever witness a pitched battle, and that my own life should depend on the issue of it: it is, indeed, mercifully ordained that we shall not see into the future. About 6, the General and his party returned. Our troops had got up to the Motee Mohul, on one side, and to the Nullah on the other, so that the two parties were only separated by a few hundred yards.

Tuesday, November 17th. The General and his Staff went out to meet Sir C—— C——. I went over to Charlie, but there was not much to be seen from his house, and there was a 24-pounder in the Dawk Office Compound, just below his window, which, when it fired, regularly blew a blast into the room, much to my annoyance. I returned to dinner; and when the General came home in the evening, he said, as he passed into the house, "Ladies, I have seen the Commander-in-Chief." The communication was now opened with our troops; some of his staff remained talking with us,[11] and we then heard that Col. N——, and Mr. S——, A.D.C., had been wounded. The General had rushed across to the Commander-in-Chief, through a heavy fire. After prayer in the evening, he called Dr. F—— aside, and said a few words to him; and when Dr. F—— came back he said: "All ladies, and the sick and wounded, are to be out of the garrison before to-morrow night, and can only take what they can carry in their hands." It came upon us like a thunderbolt; one felt almost paralysed—so helpless! How were we to go, and what could

[10] These mines were prepared by us to throw down several walls, to assist our troops in getting in.

[11] While I was talking to an officer, a bullet passed between our faces.

we take with us? We were told not to name it; out of our own garrison that night, or else I should have gone off to Charlie at once. Several of the ladies sat up all night, stitching things of value into their petticoats, &c.; I sat up a little while, but I got such an internal shivering and spasms with the start it had given me, that I was obliged to go to bed, fearing I might get one of my attacks; of course, sleep was out of the question.

Wednesday, November 18th. I got up at daybreak, and rushed over to Charlie. I found him fast asleep, but awoke him with the news, which he would not believe; however, he got up and gave me all sorts of instructions how to manage, and said he would set off and see if he could contrive anything for me. I went home again to stitch my valuables around me; and, by dinner time he had got me two old men—fathers of Sepoys who had been with us all through the siege—one of whom was to carry a bundle of bedding, and the other my dressing case; our only servant, a punkah coolie, was to carry a tin box: he cheered me with the news also, that he had got leave to accompany me as far as Secundrabagh.[12] So I must walk, having no carriage; however, there came an order that we were not to go till the next day. I was thankful, for I was quite worn out with the preparations. Charlie, also, was quite done up, he had been over so often to help me; and we are none of us very strong; and after all he brought me 2 lbs. of sugar, a great treat, for we had tasted none for weeks. We went to bed all worn out, Charlie sending word, the last thing, that I was to have the Subadar's mare to ride the next day. The Sikh cook was to carry a banghy; so I set to work and packed my little portmanteau with what next I thought I should most like to save (the difficulty was to select), and all these things went off at night with Herah Sing, a Sikh Sepoy in charge. Charlie had given him a note to Col. B— —, to take charge of them till I arrived next day; but, the Colonel was killed that very afternoon—so Capt. N— —, Assistant Adjutant-General, kindly took charge of them instead.

Thursday. November 19th. Charlie came over the first thing, and said Capt. W— — had lent him a coolie, so I had to pack another box, and as Herah Sing had invested thirty-five rupees in a pony (without orders) for me to ride, I got a side-saddle from Mrs. F— —; and then came the news that the Brigadier had cancelled Charlie's leave, as so many had been applying for the same. It gave me a sharp pang indeed, for this may be our parting in India; however, it was no time to give way, so I dressed in all the clothes I could, fearing I might not be able to get my boxes carried on from Secundrabagh. I put on three of each kind of under garments—a pink flannel dressing-gown, and plaid jacket, and then over all my cloth dress and jacket made out of my habit. I then tied my Cashmere shawl round my waist, and also Charlie's silver mug, and put on a worsted cap and hat, and had my cloak placed on the saddle; in my pink dressing gown I had stitched dear mamma's last present to me, and I filled several pockets with valuables also; in two under ones I had all my little stock of jewellery, and my journal, and some valuable papers. I also wore a bustle, in which I had stitched my Honiton lace wedding dress, veil, &c., and two black and white lace shawls; so that I was a pretty good size. At half-past 10, Charlie and Capt. W— —, with great difficulty mount-

[12] Two miles out.

ed me on my pony,—a very difficult affair dressed and laden as I was and with no spring in me. Capt. W—— and a large party, were in fits of laughter; at last it was accomplished, and Charlie took me out to the Baillie Guard Gate, and there we parted with a shake of the hands, not knowing when we might meet again! My heart was very heavy, but it was no time to give way. Herah Sing led my pony very carefully. At last we came to a part that was dangerous; the enemy commanded it from the Kaiser Bagh, and the musket shots were whistling about, so some soldiers advised my dismounting and walking through the trenches which had been cut for us. I did so; and when I came out at the engine house an officer came forward to meet me and congratulated me and offered his assistance. I said I was waiting for my pony, so he offered me his charpoy to sit on till it came round and sent his Orderly to look for it; at last it came, and he took me through some barracks to meet it, and there attempted to mount me, but of course unsuccessfully. At last, however, with the assistance of a tall soldier and Herah Sing, and a chair, I was got up again, and then he begged to know my name that he might tell my friends he had sent me on safely, and I asked to whom I was indebted for so much kindness? He said, "Mr. F——, of the Artillery;" and when I named Capt. G—— he said, "Oh! I know G—— very well, and I will be sure to tell him you are all right!" So on I went, steadily, till I came to another dangerous part, when another soldier told me I had better dismount; but I thought of my former difficulties, so I made Herah Sing double the pony across, the balls whistling over our heads. When we got to Secundrabagh, there were the 93rd Highlanders in their kilts and bonnets, and the Naval Brigade with their great guns. I spoke to one of the sailors on a 24-pounder, and asked if there were any place appropriated to the ladies? He jumped off, and said he would show me the way, and congratulated me on getting out of Lucknow, and asked if he could do anything for me? He said his name was Mr. H——, and he belonged to the *Shannon*, and that he might be found at any time at that gun if I sent for him. He then told me of the fight they had coming in, and that 1,842 Natives had been killed in that very garden; the bodies were counted as they were buried: he said they lay in heaps breast high. I took up my position in the corner of a verandah, as it was cleaner than the house. Mrs. B—— was the only lady arrived. Herah Sing drew me some water, and I took out a ham sandwich Charlie had given me in the morning—his own breakfast—for they had had a ham at the Brigade Mess, one that had been kept in store as a treat to be eaten when the relief arrived. While I was eating it, Captain C—— came up and offered to do anything for me; so I asked for a hackery to take on my baggage. He said he could give me camels, but I preferred a hackery as I might be able to sit on it if my pony broke down. He gave me some sherry, and said he would send me some bread and butter—a great treat. He left, and then came Mr. H—— again and asked if I wanted anything, and sent me a loaf of bread. I asked him to get me some ropes, in case my baggage had to go on camels, which he did; and then came Capt. C—— again with his rezie and pillow for me to sit on, and his Kitmagar with bread and butter and cold mutton and a bottle of beer. I ate a little, and then asked him to cut sandwiches for me, of the rest, for night; which he did, and I put them in my basket with the bottle of beer. About the middle of the day came Miss H—— and Mrs. S——; they had walked all the way. About an hour after, came Mrs. H—— and Mrs. B—— and her baby in a buggy; they came to my corner, and our party remained together all day. Every other place was filled with ladies and children, soldiers' wives and Crannies' wives. We were to move on to the Dil Koosha in the evening, which we were glad to hear, for the smells here were intolerable. About dusk they began to make preparations, and the place was one mass of camels, bullocks, carriages and human beings; the same outside, in front of the gateway: so great was the confusion that Capt. C——, who had been ordered to keep the road open, gave it up in despair, and came and said it was utterly impossible to do so; he had left a string of camels entangled in a ditch, and the road was one mass of entanglement; he was, however, obliged to go off again, and it became pitch dark; and there we were, left to our own devices: how we were ever to get on, none of us could tell. However, at last I decided my best plan was to load my pony with my bundle of bedding, and walk myself, and the rest of my baggage must take its chance; the coolie who had night blindness, and one of the old men, must remain with it, and get Capt. C—— to send it on in a hackery next day. I got a soldier of the 9th Lancers, named Mitchell, to load the pony for me; he was very civil, and did all he could for me: we then sat down in the dark, patiently, till we should get our orders to move; the enemy were out between us and the Dil Koosha, and we were not to go without a large escort, which was to be ready at 8. A little before that time came Capt. E——, to say the enemy were out so strong that no carriages of any kind were to go on that evening, we must hurry with all speed to the Dil Koosha, but must go a roundabout, sandy road, and must run no risk of being hindered by carriages sticking in the sand: as many dhoolies (palanquins for the sick) as could be procured would be in readiness for the ladies, and those who could not get them must walk. Soon after, fortunately, came up Mr. O'D——, who said our only plan would be to go and take possession of empty dhoolies ourselves; so off we set, he dragging us through the entangled mass—far worse than any London mob—and he put us into four dhoolies, nearly all separated. I called to my old man to bring the pony and bundle of bedding, but that was utterly impossible for the time; we waited some time in the dhoolies, and then mine and Miss H——'s were ordered somewhere to the front, but in quite a different direction to what I considered the right road to the Dil Koosha. We heard the enemy firing in the distance: never shall I forget the confusion of that night—the masses crowded together in the pitch darkness; for even when Mrs. B—— had a candle lighted, thinking her baby was dying (its breath having been caught by the cold air), it was ordered to be put out immediately, on account of the number of ammunition waggons. I think we must have started about 9; we went on steadily for some distance, and then some of the advanced guard came riding back, telling the dhoolie-bearers not to speak a word, the enemy were so near; so on we went, nothing to be heard but the tramp of the bearers; after a time we were all halted, and not allowed to make the slightest noise, the enemy were so close. After a time, on we went again in silence, a very roundabout way, and when I looked at my watch after our arrival, I found it had stopped at ten minutes past 2. Now, the direct road would only have been two miles. We were kept waiting on our arrival for some time, for they said there was no place ready for us; we were turned back from the house, as there were already 1,100 sick there. After waiting about an hour in the cold, I seized a gentleman who was passing with a lantern, and asked him where we were to go; he pointed to some tents a long way off, and after tumbling over innumerable tent-pegs and ropes we reached them, and lay down on the ground for the night—for it was utterly impossible to find my pony with the bedding—but we got a rizie (quilt) to lie upon, and I put my head on my basket. The tents were so open that I, of course, got a severe cold; however, daylight soon appeared.

Friday, November 20th. As soon as day dawned I went all over the immense camp in search of my pony. I found several ladies had passed the night in their dhoolies; Mrs. B—— fortunately had a small tent of her own, so she went straight off to the commissariat officer and asked him for a place for it, and kindly asked me to share it with her; it was such a luxury, when it was pitched, to get into it by ourselves, and I had found the pony, with my bedding, so when I was dressed I lay down on it and rested, for I felt quite worn out. We spent the day quietly; in the afternoon, to our great delight, Mr. C—— brought us a packet of overland letters. Oh! the joy of having them once again, and finding all our dear ones at home were well; we had received none for many months. My hackery arrived, just after, with my worldly goods; Capt. C—— had kindly sent them on from Secundrabagh, so that I began to feel more comfortable. We went to bed very early, to recruit our strength.

Saturday, November 21st. I rose early, and took home some newspapers that had been lent me, in one of which was an account of poor Mrs. B——'s murder at Hissar. On our return we drew our rations—bread, meat, tea, sugar, rice, dal, and salt—a bountiful supply: I then sent off the coolie to Charlie with a note, and he sent me back a charpoy (bed) and some other things, so I had no longer to sleep on the ground.

Sunday, November 22nd. A quiet day! But we have no service, although there were six Padres in the camp. In the evening, to our joy, we heard the old garrison were leaving Lucknow, and might be with us that night. Mrs. B—— and I sat up till Davie came and told us they could not be here till the next morning.

Monday, November 23rd. Rose early, and went out to enquire for our husbands, and found they had arrived, but were kept in a camp, about a mile off. We waited impatiently till 4 P.M., when Mr. B—— made his appearance; he said he had waited all day, to ask the Brigadier's leave to come up; but the Brigadier had been away himself all day with his wife; so he set off without leave, and met him just returning. About sunset, in came dear Charlie, limping sadly; he was loaded with a sword, carbine, haversack, case bottle, and a stick to help him along; he had gone on the sick list, for his knee was so bad, he did not feel equal to marching. He had tea with us, and then stretched his bedding outside our tent, under the awning of it, so as to escape the dew; but I longed to give him shelter, it was so cold. We packed all ready for starting, as we were to march in the morning; but the hour was kept secret, on account of the enemy.

Tuesday, November 24th. Charlie called us at 6, thinking we should be off early: however, we did not start till noon. All the ladies were ordered to collect in front of the Commander-in-Chief's tents, when all those who had no private carriages, would be stowed away in covered hackeries: the dhoolies were all kept for the sick. We were late, for Mrs. B—— would not leave in her buggy till the Bheestie was ready to accompany her. I mounted my pony, and we tried, with Charlie's assistance, to make our way through long lines of baggage, hackeries, camels, bullocks, &c., &c.; never, I believe, was such a scene! The whole army marched, excepting a few to keep the Dil Kooshe for a short time. There were 1,000 sick carried in dhoolies, and 467 women and children, in any kind of conveyance that could be got for them, added to Sir C——'s whole army, a portion of which consisted of nine batteries: never shall I forget the scene! As far as the eye could reach, on all sides were strings of vehicles, elephants, camels, &c., &c.; and when we were all pitched for the night, our camp extended over seven miles. The dhoolies were all kept for the sick; none were allowed even to ladies who were hourly expecting their confinement: Sir C—— said the wounded men must be first thought of, as they had saved our lives. The dust was overpowering! We went across country to avoid the enemy. Our road was over cultivated fields; such ups and downs! It was a wonder how the vehicles surmounted them. Most of the carriages were drawn by bullocks, as the horses had been too much weakened by the siege to be of any service. Being such tremendous lines, we were frequently stopped by entanglements; and though we had only four or five miles to go, we did not get to our ground till dark. The number of guns with the force added immensely to the number of vehicles accompanying us. As I said before, we had nine batteries, the Naval Brigade included, and the Artillery park and magazine attached is tremendous. There were also innumerable commissariat carts, and many with treasure from Lucknow, the Commander-in-Chief with one division, and General O—— with another. General H—— died this day of dysentery. We heard distant firing all the way, and hoped it was not on the little party left at the Dil Koosha. I could not possibly describe the confusion when we arrived at our encamping ground for the night. I had been obliged to get off my pony, as the sun was so powerful, and get into a hackery, and "squat" down on the straw, like most of the other ladies; but when we got to the ground, we had to hunt about for our baggage, the little we had brought with us. Luckily, Charlie got hold of our baggage hackery, and got down my charpoy for me to sit on; but it was bitterly cold, so that Mrs. B—— took her baby into some officer's tent till her own could be found. We had brought a little bread and meat in a cooking vessel—our day's rations; also tea and sugar. I had purchased some cheese at the Dil Koosha, so Mrs. B——'s Ayah, a Musselmaunee, set to work and boiled the kettle on the ground, and then fried the beef in a little frying pan I had brought, and we had a grand tea: beef, and bread and cheese, and tea with milk and sugar in it. It revived us a little, but poor Charlie seemed quite done up; and poor Mrs. B—— had been nursing her baby all day, without taking anything herself. Luckily, up came Mr. B—— with her camels and tent; he had been searching for them: it was soon pitched, and we were in luxury compared with most; for many poor delicate women and children passed the night on the ground, by the side of their hackeries, and the nights are bitterly cold now. The hackeries were too full for all to lie down in them. Charlie put his bedding partly under the awning of some tent, to escape the dew, which is very heavy; and it is very dangerous sleeping in it.

Wednesday, November 25th. We halted—and really needed it. Charlie drew his own rations, and we had all our meals together, and got on very happily though not in great comfort. Mrs. B——'s Ayah did all the cooking for us, and made some delicious pourries for tea. We went to bed at 8, very tired. Charlie slept this night in a dhoolie.

Thursday, November 26th. We expected an order to march, but did not get it; a party of the 8th Queen's and some Engineers went on ahead to repair the Bunnee bridge for us, so we halted this day also.

Friday, November 27th. An order was given for us to march at 7 A.M., but just as we had prepared everything for starting we were told we were not to go till after breakfast. About 11 we started, and went about thirteen miles, encamping for the night two miles on the Cawnpore side of Bunnee. I was very tired with the jolting of the hackery.

Saturday, November 28th. While we were still in bed, came an order to strike tents and be off; it seemed almost more than one could do: we hurried and dressed, and had a little breakfast, and I was in the hackery by 8! We had tremendous work to get out of the crowd of hackeries starting and get into the line, and it was half-past 9 before we really began our march. We heard very heavy firing at Cawnpore all day, so that the Chief ordered us not to halt at Enown, but march the whole way in to the banks of the river—thirty miles—he himself hurried on to Cawnpore, and it was fortunate he did, for the Gwalior mutineers had been there three days; and this day, the 64th Queen's, returning from spiking some guns, lost 7 or 8 officers; indeed, all that went out with them: and an officer of the 70th had to bring them out of action. I jolted on in my hackney from 8 in the morning till 12 at night, the life almost jolted out of me; luckily we had bread and cheese and a bottle of beer with us. Charlie dragged on his weary way, first walking and then in the hackery, but he was quite done up at last; and yet, when we got to the encamping ground, we were two hours more searching for Mrs. B——'s tent: it was 2 o'clock before I got in. Then, of course, our baggage hackery never arrived till late the next day; so we had to contrive and boil a little water in a lotah, so as to have a cup of tea, and then we lay down,—Charlie outside and I in the tent with Mrs. B——.

Sunday, November 29th. We hoped to be allowed to halt, but an order came that we were to go two miles nearer the river, and to form a very compact camp on account of the enemy. We started again, and got to camp in the middle of the day; had the tent pitched in a nice turfy spot, and were having dinner all comfortably, when another order came that we were to cross the river that night! This was killing work, but we afterwards heard the enemy intended firing on the bridge of boats; luckily, Sir Colin had a battery up close to it, and kept them off. No doubt it was a most anxious time to him—but we did grumble occasionally, as he did not appear to think much of our comfort. Mrs. S—— was confined in her dhoolie while changing ground this morning. At 8 P.M. we started—all the baggage hackeries were to be stopped for us ladies to cross the bridge of boats; but in consequence of some of them having "dodged" into the line, it took us eight hours to do the three miles; fortunately, it was a splendid moonlight night; just as we were on the bridge of boats there was a sudden discharge of musketry, which greatly alarmed us. I thought for certain the enemy were going to attack us, but it turned out to be our own men firing in the entrenchment; we happened to have stuck just at the time, and the bridge of boats is so narrow we could not have escaped. I own I was more frightened this night than any time during the siege; however, we got safely to the Artillery barracks, where we were to halt; some very dirty crannies had taken possession before us. However, we lay down on our bedding which we had brought in the hackery with us and slept till 8 A.M.

Monday, November 30th. We waited on in misery till the tent came up, which was not till late in the day, and then we found the Bheesti, our factotum, had fever, and could not work; however, Charlie managed to get the tent partly up, when another order came to move to some other barracks half a mile off. In the midst of it all, Charlie contrived to hurt his bad knee against a tent-peg. Some started for these new barracks, and we were preparing, when a counter-order came that we were to wait till morning; so we got our tent up, and slept in it.

Tuesday, December 1st. We took our chota hazree, and then went to our new quarters, where we pitched our tent, and made ourselves comfortable, and we were actually allowed to remain in peace for the rest of the day.

Wednesday, December 2nd. We hoped to remain in peace, and the Brigadier asked Charlie what sort of an appointment he would like; but, unluckily, he was totally unfit for work, and so obliged to decline all. About sunset came an order for us to march that night (we had just returned from visiting General W——'s entrenchments), and no gentlemen were to accompany us but Captains E—— and B——. Charlie had not yet got his sick certificate from Dr. C——, so I was in a sad state of mind, fearing we must now separate altogether. We set to work dividing our clothes, &c., as best we could, but we were both excessively tired. I did not lie down till 12, midnight, and then did so fully dressed, expecting every moment to be ordered off. I had a most distracting headache; however, the night passed on, and we did not move.

Thursday, December 3rd. I woke Charlie at daybreak, and he went off to the superintending surgeon, to see if he would sign his papers, and then was told to come at noon: at noon he went, and did not return till 4, when he said he had got his certificate. I was overjoyed. We marched at 10 P.M.; I went in a shigram with a Mrs R——, Charlie seated on the step, and Mr. R—— in front. Charlie guided the blind coolie with my pony all night by holding his stick out to him, and the coolie taking the other end of it. I was more idle, for I slept all night. We went twenty-five miles.

Friday, December 4th. All very fatigued this morning, Mrs. B—— especially. We got a couple of delicious chickens and some eggs for dinner, a treat we had not enjoyed for months. We were ordered to march at 9 P.M. Mr. R—— had had fever all day, so I gave up my place in the shigram to him, and Charlie and I travelled in the hackery. We went thirteen miles this night.

Saturday, December 5th. I felt quite stiff and bruised by the jolting in the hackery. We asked Mr. C—— to bring his rations, and we would cook them with ours, as he had no servants and got hardly anything yesterday; he says the amount of misery experienced by the wounded travelling in the rough hackeries is hardly credible, and many did not get their wounds dressed or have anything to eat the whole day. There is a sad want of servants and management. We started again at 7 P.M., having had our hackery well littered with straw, and went twenty-four miles, not stopping at Futtehpore, which was half way.

Sunday, December 6th. We got to camp about 9 A.M.; the tents were pitched in a nice tope of trees. We were ordered on again at 9 P.M., and had rather a long march; the last mile of it we turned off the trunk road over a rough track to the railroad, of which we knew nothing, as we both slept, and on awakening found ourselves at the temporary terminus.

Monday, December 7th. We hoped to breakfast before we left the ground; but no, we were packed into the railway carriages immediately, and then were kept waiting three hours for the baggage to be loaded. Charlie gave up all hope of being able to accompany us, it was such a time before he could find our baggage and get it into the train; but it was done at last. We took three hours getting to Allahabad, stopping once to water the engine, which in this enlightened country is done by coolies with earthen jars—the apparatus not being in order. We luckily had a bottle of porter and some Native biscuits, so we kept up till we arrived at Allahabad at 3 P.M., where we met with a most unexpected reception, the whole station being lined with gentlemen and soldiers who turned out for the occasion, and cheered us most lustily; it was almost overpowering. They had done everything they could for our comfort; all sorts of vehicles had been lent by their owners to take us from the station to the fort, where a large suite of the Governor-General's tents, about fifteen in number, had been pitched for us. We shared a double-poled tent with Captain and Mrs. R——; it had one public and two private compartments. It was a great luxury to be quiet by ourselves, after the many months we had been herded together. Captain D—— sent us over a splendid dinner. We met Dr. H—— and S—— H—— at the station; all the former could do was to squeeze my hand and say "Poor thing! poor thing!" Our tents were very comfortably furnished; so, after taking tea with the R——'s, we went to bed.

Tuesday, December 8th. It was such luxury to be in bed, and have my chota hazree brought to me, after having had to make it for so many months—almost the whole of the siege—and it was such delicious bread and butter! Mr. S——, the chaplain, and some gentlemen, came round to all the tents, early, bringing cakes of soap for us; and the night before all our tents were supplied with oil lamps. We went over to breakfast in the Mess tent—it was the Governor-General's Durbar tent—a most splendid one, and pitched in the centre of our camp; we had a delicious breakfast—coffee, with rich cream. I enjoyed it much, after our siege fare, and was as pleased as a child to get it. We telegraphed to Capt. P——, in Calcutta, to write home, and say we were all safe. Drs. B—— and H——, and Major T—— called. After this, our days passed quietly at Allahabad. Christmas Day, we dined with Capt. J——, of the Fusiliers; and Monday, January 11th, left Allahabad in country boats, to join the steamers at Sirsa, as none of them could come up higher, on account of the shallow water on the Dum-dumma Flats. We had a narrow escape! As our boat was alongside the *Charles Allen*, another steamer passed, having several Native boats attached to its flat; one came with great force against ours, and every one expected we were done for, as these Native boats generally crush up and go down instantaneously. There was a cry, "Save the women and children!" and we were dragged up on the top of the paddle-box by our arms; however, our boat did not go down, or we must have gone with it. Captain F——, of the *Charles Allen,* afterwards told me he had expected to see us go down, and thought the poor creatures had escaped Lucknow only to meet with another horrible death. We had a pleasant trip down the river, and reached Calcutta on Thursday, January 28th. We slept that night on board, and the next morning took up our abode at 3, Harrington Street—one of the houses prepared by the Relief Fund Committee for the Lucknow refugees, where we found everything provided for us in the most luxurious style.

RETURN OF KILLED AND WOUNDED.

RETURN OF KILLED AND WOUNDED—GARRISON OF LUCKNOW, FROM 30TH JUNE TO 26TH SEPTEMBER, 1857.																				
DETAILS.	EUROPEANS.												NATIVES.							
	Killed and Died of Wounds.						Wounded.						Killed and Died of Wounds.				Wounded.			
	Officers.	Vet Surgeons.	Warrant and Staff Sergeants.	Sergeants.	Rank and File.	Total.	Officers.	Vet Surgeons.	Warrant and Staff Sergeants.	Sergeants.	Rank and File.	Total.	Native Officers.	Sergeants.	Rank and File.	Total.	Native Officers.	Sergeants.	Rank and File.	Total.
General and Brigade Staff	1	...	...	...	...	1	3	...	...	...	...	3	...	...	...	...	...	...	...	...
Artillery, Regular and Irregular	2	...	2	6	14	24	6	...	2	6	11	25	...	3	8	11	1	2	7	10
Engineers	2	...	2	...	...	4	...	...	1	...	...	1	...	...	...	...	...	...	...	...
7th Regt. Light Cavalry	2	1	1	...	...	4	1	...	...	...	...	1	...	...	...	...	...	...	...	...
H.M. 32nd Regt. of Foot	3	...	...	9	71	83	6	...	...	15	118	139	...	...	...	...	...	...	...	...
H.M. 84th Regt. of Foot, detachment	...	...	...	2	10	12	1	...	...	...	2	3	...	...	...	...	...	...	...	...
H.C. 13th Regt. N.I.	2	...	...	...	...	2	1	...	...	...	1	2	2	5	21	28	7	9	36	52
H.C. 41st Regt. N.I.	...	...	1	...	...	1	3	...	...	...	...	3	...	...	5	5	...	...	...	...
H.C. 48th Regt. N.I.	...	...	...	...	...	...	5	1	...	...	...	6	...	2	1	3	1	2	4	7
H.C. 71st Regt. N.I.	...	...	1	...	...	1	1	1	...	...	...	2	1	2	6	9	1	6	5	12
Oude Irregular Force	2	...	...	...	...	2	5	...	...	...	...	5	...	1	2	3	...	3	10	13

Native Pensioners	...	...	...	...	...	...	...	...	...	...	...	...	...	2	7	9	...	15	16	31
Native Levies	...	...	...	...	...	...	...	...	...	...	...	...	1	...	1	2	...	...	4	4
Lucknow Magazine Men	...	...	3	...	...	3	...	...	...	...	...	...	...	...	2	2	...	...	2	2
Officers not attached to the Brigade	2	...	...	...	...	2	1	...	...	...	...	1	...	...	...	...	...	...	...	...
Grand Total	16	1	10	17	95	139	33	2	3	21	132	191	4	15	53	72	10	37	84	131

N.B.—1 Member C.S. killed and 3 wounded; 1 Chaplain wounded; 2 Civil Engineers wounded; 15 Merchants, Clerks, &c., killed and 9 wounded.

Memo.—Deaths from Sickness not included.

9 789358 007817

Printed by Libri Plureos GmbH in Hamburg,
Germany